AERODATA INTERNATIONAL

MODERN U.S. FIGHTERS

Volume 1

F-14 Tomcat ● F-15 Eagle ● F-16 Fighting Falcon
F-4 Phantom II ● F-100 Super Sabre ● F-104 Starfighter

 squadron/signal publications

Published 1982 by Squadron/Signal Publications, Inc.
1115 Crowley Drive
Carrollton, Texas 75006

ISBN 0-89747-125-3

Printed in Hong Kong

McDONNELL DOUGLAS F-15 EAGLE

By Philip J. R. Moyes

Fig. 1   *An Eagle armed with Sparrow and Sidewinder missiles pictured inside a hardened shelter at one of USAFE's tactical bases. All photos courtesy of McDonnell Douglas.*

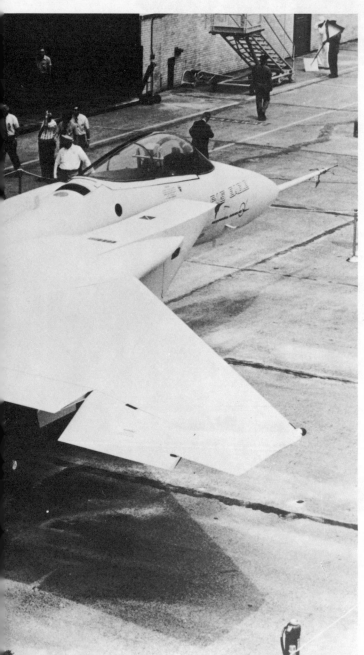

Fig. 2 *Echelon starboard formation of F-15As from the 49th and (rearmost) 58th Tactical Fighter Wings based respectively at Holloman AFB, New Mexico and Luke AFB, Arizona.* Fig. 3 *First of eighteen F-15A development aircraft, July 1972.*

Designed primarily to excel in the air-to-air combat role, the Mach 2·5-plus (1,650mph/2660km/h) McDonnell Douglas F-15 Eagle is currently the USAF's best operational fighter aeroplane – and, indeed, probably the world's best. Due to its unparalleled manoeuvrability and acceleration coupled with a highly capable all-weather weapon system, including state-of-the-art radar, fire-control and electronic counter-measures (ECM) systems, it has been hailed as the answer to any aircraft likely to be a threat in the forseeable future.

This classic air superiority fighter started out as a proposal from McDonnell Douglas' St Louis, Missouri, Division in a major design competition staged by the USAF in 1967 and also involving Fairchild Hiller and North American Rockwell. The St Louis firm was declared winner in December of that year and initially 20 development F-15s were ordered comprising 18 single-seat F-15As and two two-seat TF-15A trainers, the latter type subsequently being redesignated F-15B; the first of each type flew on 27 July 1972 and 7 July 1973 respectively. Following extensive trials, which proved beyond doubt that the F-15 was capable of fulfilling its tasks, McDonnell Douglas was authorised in March 1973 to build an initial batch of 30 production F-15s, the first of which (a two-seater) was ceremonially accepted by President Ford at Luke AFB, Arizona, on 14 November 1974. The Eagle entered operational service with Tactical Air Command at Langley AFB, Virginia, on 9 January 1976, and in the following June the USAF took delivery of its 100th Eagle. Many more have since been built and today, within the USAF, the type also serves with the United States Air Forces in Europe (USAFE), and Pacific Air Forces (PACAF). It also flies with the Israeli Air Force (whose first Eagles were four reworked development aircraft received in April 1977) and will join the Japanese Air Self-Defense Force and the Royal Saudi Air Force in mid-1980 and mid-1981 respectively.

Fig. 4 *An F-15 development machine armed with eighteen bombs and four Sparrow missiles.*

Fig. 5 *Second F-15B two-seater development aircraft, originally known as the TF-15A.*

Fig. 6 *This unpainted Eagle, the 17th development F-15A (tail number 20119), set eight world time-to-height records in January/February 1975, but some have since been broken by Russia's E-266M, a special MiG-25 Foxbat.*

The F-15 is much the same size as its older McDonnell Douglas relative the F-4 Phantom although the F-15A's normal take-off weight is more than 6,000lb (2,722kg) lighter than that of the F-4E. Powerplant is two 25,000lb (11,340kg) thrust class Pratt & Whitney F100 reheated turbofans, which, because their total thrust exceeds the aircraft's weight, enable the F-15 to climb straight up — and to do it rapidly. When, early in 1975, a specially prepared Eagle known as the *Streak Eagle* set eight world time-to-height records, it ran up its engines while stopped on a runway and then shot to over 39,000ft (11,887m) in less than one minute. When it stopped climbing it was more than 103,000ft (31,395m) above the ground. Some of these records have since been broken by Russia's E-266M, a special MiG-25 *Foxbat.*

Fig. 7 *Compare this view of a Sparrow AAM and bomb-carrying F-15A development aircraft with Fig 4. Engine air intakes of the Eagle are hinged across their lower surfaces and rotate automatically so that they always face directly into the airflow. F-15 is first aircraft to feature directional intakes, which are necessary to guide the air smoothly through quite large changes of direction on its way to the engines.*

Fig. 8 *First F-15C (tail number 78-468) which first flew on 26 February 1979.*

Most F-15s are single seaters (the F-15A and F-15C) but about 15 per cent have two seats (F-15B and F-15D) so they can function as trainers in addition to being capable of combat. The versions are identical externally, except that the two-seaters have slightly larger canopies. The F-15C and D supplanted the A and B models on the production lines during June 1979 and differ in having programmable radar signal processors giving a fourfold increase in computer capacity, plus the ability to continue tracking one target while searching for others, and to transfer radar lock-on from one target to another. Both the F-15C and D are able to carry FAST Packs (Fuel And Sensor Tactical Packs) which are conformal aerodynamically-shaped pallets which attach to the sides of the engine air intakes and can hold 10,000lb (4,536kg) of fuel or 227 cubic feet (6,428 cubic metres) of avionics and other equipment.

When extra tanks carrying 12,000lb (5,443kg) more fuel are added, the F-15C and D's maximum fuel load is 35,000lb (15,876kg) or more than 5,400 US gallons (4,493 Imp gal). The Eagle's remarkable fuel capacity results in an extremely long range. With fuel capacity increased by FAST Packs it has on several occasions flown non-stop and unrefuelled from the USA to Europe.

Fig. 9 *Testing of the FAST Pack was undertaken by the second F-15B development machine (10291). When this photo was taken the aircraft was also carrying a 600-US gallon (2,273 litre) fuel tank on the fuselage strong point plus two more such tanks on wing pylons.*

Fig. 10 *Pair of F-15As of the 32nd TFS based at Soesterberg, in Holland, patrol the north European skies. Full Sparrow and Sidewinder armament is seen to advantage on the banking Eagle.*

When speed is called for, as when enemy attack aircraft must be intercepted, the Eagle can deliver at Mach 2·5-plus, whilst at the other end of the speed range, it can maintain controlled flight at less than 115mph (185km/h). Its low wing loading and ability to endure many Gs – it has been tested to more than nine Gs (where the 200lb/90kg man would weigh 1,800lb/810kg) – make the Eagle extraordinarily manoeuvrable.

Standard armament of the Eagle is an internal, wing-mounted 20mm rapid-firing cannon and short and long-range missiles. For combat with distant aircraft, the F-15 combines long-range Hughes radar with four AIM-7F advanced Sparrow missiles, which latter are carried

on the lower fuselage corners. The AIM-7F is an all-aspect, long-range, high-speed, all-weather, radar-guided missile with advanced solid-state systems assuring accuracy and reliability. It is two to three times more effective than its predecessor, the AIM-7E. USAF pilots flew their Eagles in engagements over Edwards AFB, California, against aircraft flying too far away to be seen and simulating the planes of potential enemies. Some of the F-15's adversaries in these exercises were less capable aircraft, but many were quite advanced and fully able to engage in air-to-air combat. One hundred and thirty-seven engagements ocurred during the tests, and not one F-15 was declared lost. The Eagles consistently detected the threat aircraft and fired first. Even

Fig. 11 *All-aspect, long-range, high-speed, all-weather AIM-7F Sparrow AAM, seen here being fired from an F-15A, has advanced solid-state systems ensuring accuracy and reliability, and is two to three times more effective than its predecessor, the AIM-7E.*

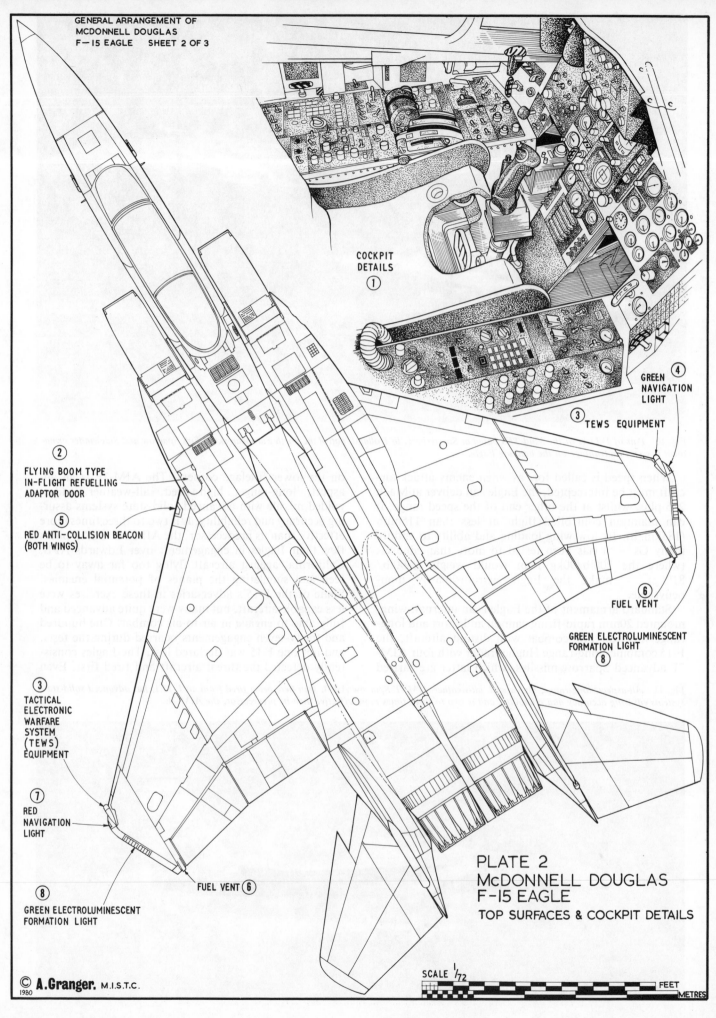

COCKPIT
DETAILS
①

②
FLYING BOOM TYPE
IN-FLIGHT REFUELLING
ADAPTOR DOOR

⑤
RED ANTI-COLLISION BEACON
(BOTH WINGS)

③
TACTICAL
ELECTRONIC
WARFARE
SYSTEM
(TEWS)
EQUIPMENT

⑦
RED
NAVIGATION
LIGHT

⑧
GREEN ELECTROLUMINESCENT
FORMATION LIGHT

FUEL VENT ⑥

④
GREEN
NAVIGATION
LIGHT

③ TEWS EQUIPMENT

⑥
FUEL VENT

⑧
GREEN ELECTROLUMINESCENT
FORMATION LIGHT

PLATE 2
McDONNELL DOUGLAS
F—15 EAGLE
TOP SURFACES & COCKPIT DETAILS

© A.Granger. M.I.S.T.C.
1980

SCALE 1/72   FEET
METRES

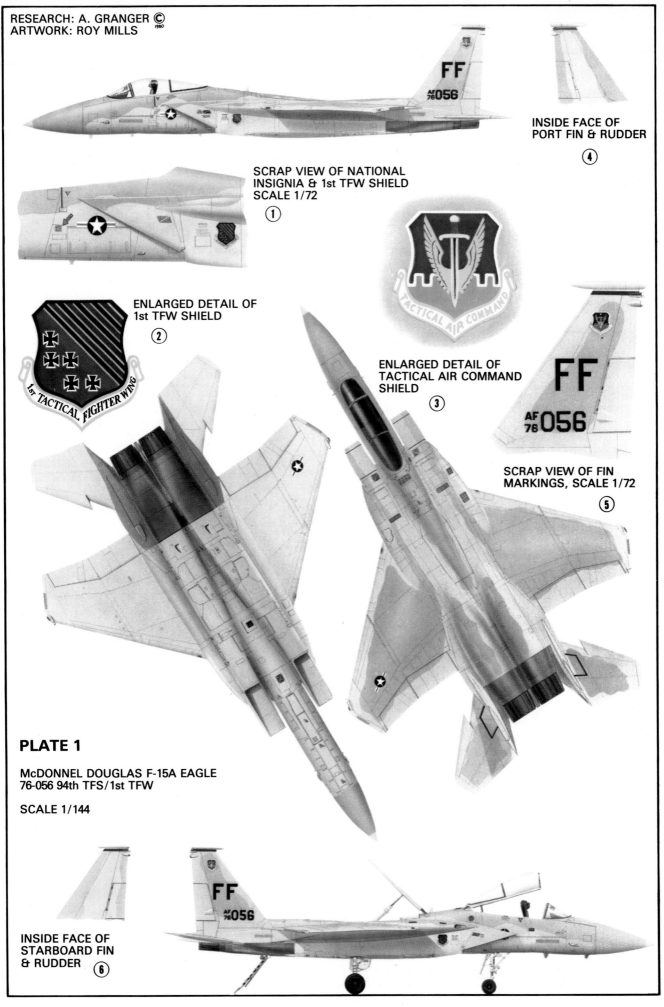

RESEARCH: A. GRANGER ©1980
ARTWORK: ROY MILLS

INSIDE FACE OF
PORT FIN & RUDDER
④

SCRAP VIEW OF NATIONAL
INSIGNIA & 1st TFW SHIELD
SCALE 1/72
①

ENLARGED DETAIL OF
1st TFW SHIELD
②

ENLARGED DETAIL OF
TACTICAL AIR COMMAND
SHIELD
③

SCRAP VIEW OF FIN
MARKINGS, SCALE 1/72
⑤

PLATE 1

McDONNEL DOUGLAS F-15A EAGLE
76-056 94th TFS/1st TFW

SCALE 1/144

INSIDE FACE OF
STARBOARD FIN
& RUDDER
⑥

9

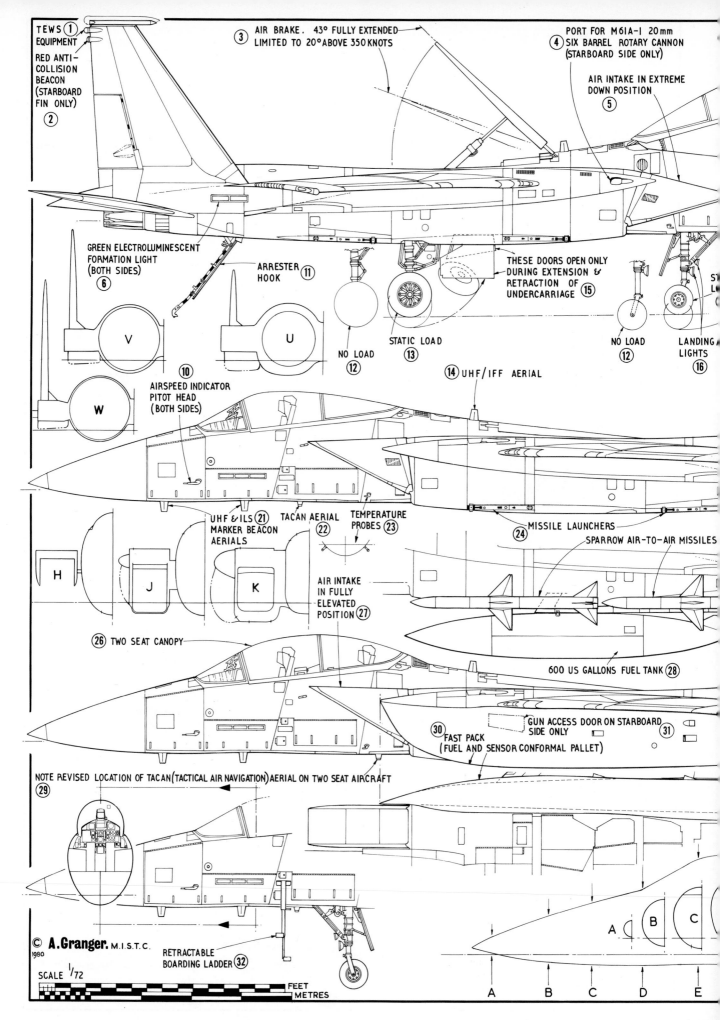

TEWS ① EQUIPMENT

RED ANTI-COLLISION BEACON (STARBOARD FIN ONLY) ②

③ AIR BRAKE. 43° FULLY EXTENDED LIMITED TO 20° ABOVE 350 KNOTS

PORT FOR M61A-1 20mm ④ SIX BARREL ROTARY CANNON (STARBOARD SIDE ONLY)

AIR INTAKE IN EXTREME DOWN POSITION ⑤

GREEN ELECTROLUMINESCENT FORMATION LIGHT (BOTH SIDES) ⑥

ARRESTER HOOK ⑪

THESE DOORS OPEN ONLY DURING EXTENSION & RETRACTION OF UNDERCARRIAGE ⑮

V   U

W

NO LOAD ⑫

STATIC LOAD ⑬

NO LOAD ⑫

LANDING LIGHTS ⑯

⑩ AIRSPEED INDICATOR PITOT HEAD (BOTH SIDES)

⑭ UHF/IFF AERIAL

H   J   K

UHF & ILS ㉑ MARKER BEACON AERIALS

TACAN AERIAL ㉒

TEMPERATURE PROBES ㉓

MISSILE LAUNCHERS ㉔

SPARROW AIR-TO-AIR MISSILES

AIR INTAKE IN FULLY ELEVATED POSITION ㉗

㉖ TWO SEAT CANOPY

600 US GALLONS FUEL TANK ㉘

㉚ FAST PACK (FUEL AND SENSOR CONFORMAL PALLET)

GUN ACCESS DOOR ON STARBOARD SIDE ONLY   ㉛

NOTE REVISED LOCATION OF TACAN (TACTICAL AIR NAVIGATION) AERIAL ON TWO SEAT AIRCRAFT ㉙

© A. Granger. M.I.S.T.C.
1980

RETRACTABLE BOARDING LADDER ㉜

SCALE 1/72

FEET
METRES

A   B   C   D   E

A   B   C

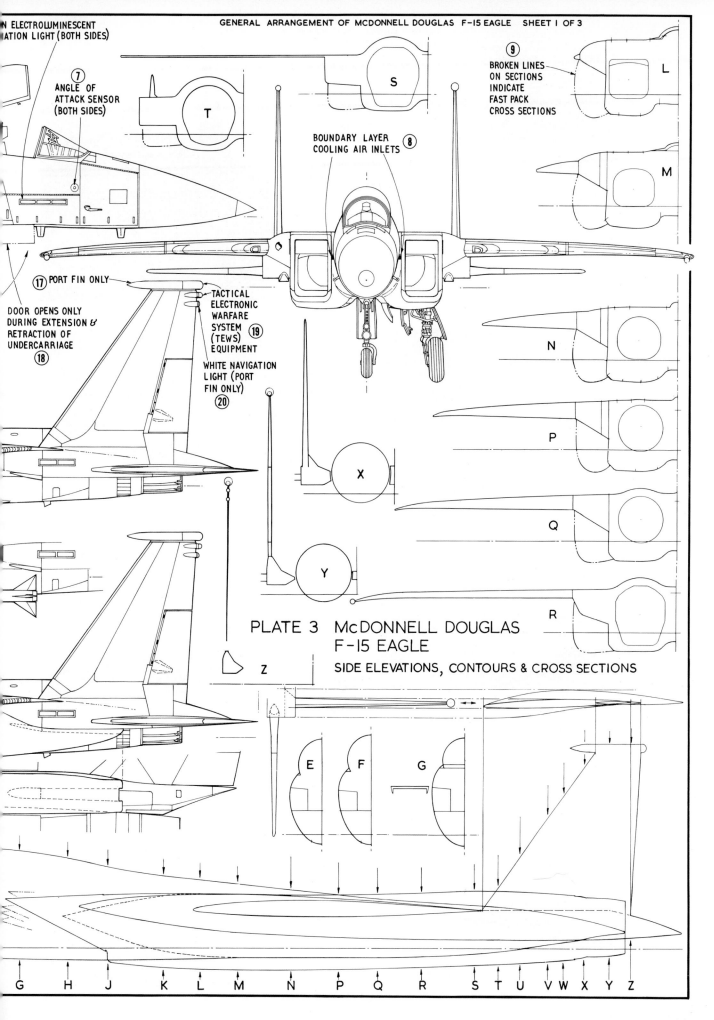

ELECTROLUMINESCENT
ATION LIGHT (BOTH SIDES)

⑦ ANGLE OF
ATTACK SENSOR
(BOTH SIDES)

⑨ BROKEN LINES
ON SECTIONS
INDICATE
FAST PACK
CROSS SECTIONS

L

M

BOUNDARY LAYER
COOLING AIR INLETS ⑧

S

T

⑰ PORT FIN ONLY

TACTICAL
ELECTRONIC
WARFARE
SYSTEM ⑲
(TEWS)
EQUIPMENT

WHITE NAVIGATION
LIGHT (PORT
FIN ONLY)
⑳

DOOR OPENS ONLY
DURING EXTENSION &
RETRACTION OF
UNDERCARRIAGE
⑱

N

P

Q

R

X

Y

Z

PLATE 3 McDONNELL DOUGLAS
F-15 EAGLE

SIDE ELEVATIONS, CONTOURS & CROSS SECTIONS

E   F   G

G   H   J   K   L   M   N   P   Q   R   S   T   U   V   W   X   Y   Z

11

Fig. 13 *An Eagle carrying four Sparrow missiles, four Sidewinder missiles and a 600-US gallon (2,273 litre) auxiliary fuel tank.* Fig. 14 *F-15A 74-091 of the 36th TFW, Bitburg, W Germany.* Fig. 15 *F-15As 74-093 and 74-091 of the 27th TFS/1st TFW, Langley AFB, Virginia.* Fig. 16 *F-15As of the 58th TFTW, Luke AFB, Arizona.* Fig. 17 *Essential mission information is projected on a head-up display. Often-used switches are on the stick, throttle and directly below the HUD.* Fig. 18 *F-15A 77-082 of the 32nd TFS, Soesterberg, Holland.* Fig. 19 *F-15B 76-139 of the 49th TFW, Holloman AFB, New Mexico.* Fig. 20 *Two F-15As of the 58th TFTW over the Arizona Desert.*

13

17

14

18

15

19

16

20

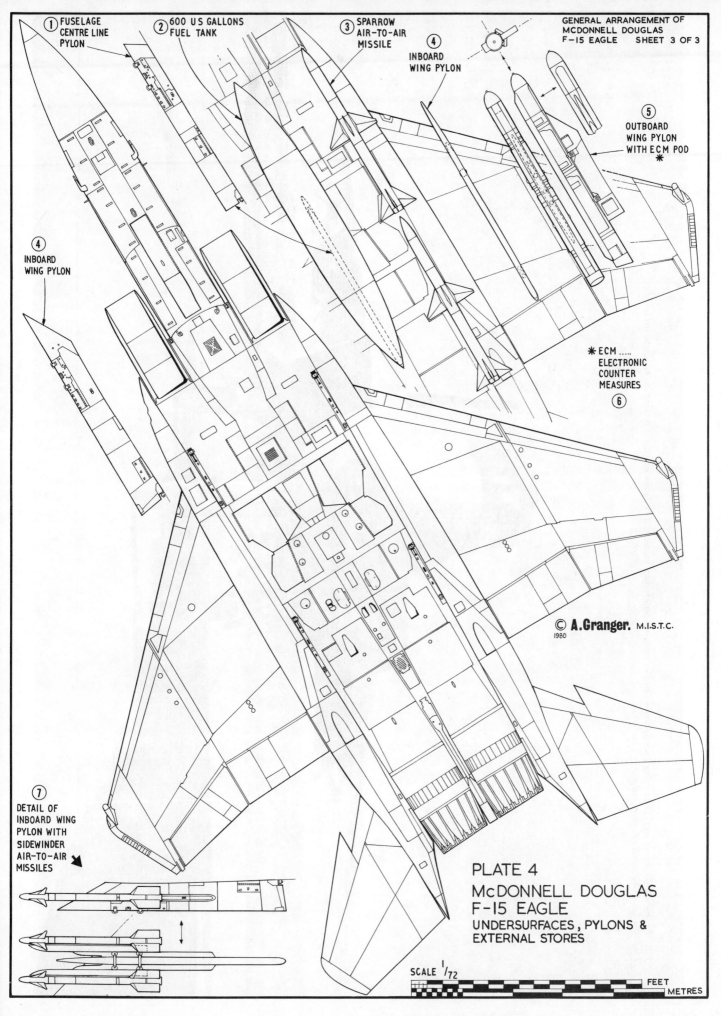

① FUSELAGE CENTRE LINE PYLON

② 600 US GALLONS FUEL TANK

③ SPARROW AIR-TO-AIR MISSILE

④ INBOARD WING PYLON

⑤ OUTBOARD WING PYLON WITH ECM POD ✱

④ INBOARD WING PYLON

✱ ECM ..... ELECTRONIC COUNTER MEASURES

⑥

© A.Granger. M.I.S.T.C.
1980

⑦ DETAIL OF INBOARD WING PYLON WITH SIDEWINDER AIR-TO-AIR MISSILES

PLATE 4
McDONNELL DOUGLAS
F-15 EAGLE
UNDERSURFACES, PYLONS & EXTERNAL STORES

SCALE 1/72

FEET
METRES

13

Fig. 12   *Head-on view of an F-15 carrying four Sparrow missiles and four Sidewinder missiles. The 20mm cannon is housed in the starboard wing root and has 940 rounds of ammunition.*

Fig. 21 *Eighth F-15A development aircraft (10287) seen in profile.* Fig. 22 *Second development F-15B (10291) with FAST Pack low-drag fuel and sensor pallets installed.*

when electronic jamming equipment was used in an attempt to blind the Eagles, the F-15 pilots engaged and defeated their foes.

Air Force officers at Eglin AFB, Florida, tested the F-15 against high-altitude, high-speed threats – drones, flying at 2.7 times the speed of sound near 70,000ft (21,335m), simulating Russia's most formidable fighter, the MiG-25 *Foxbat*. The F-15s succeeded. Shortly afterwards, over the test range at China Lake, California, F-15s were pitted against low-flying, manoeuvrable targets and again did the job. Thorough air superiority testing also included one-to-one engagements between F-15s and a wide variety of adversary aircraft – and the Eagles won all but two of the 178 engagements.

The Eagle has also demonstrated its all-weather capability by detecting and defeating F-4s and F-111s under adverse weather conditions in NATO European exercises involving the Airborne Warning and Control System (AWACS). A single F-15 was involved in the 10-day test, which was marked by what turned out to be

mostly poor weather, and during that time it didn't miss a single sortie. It intercepted two F-111s penetrating Britain from the north, its radar detecting the first at a range of 100 miles (161km). Those targets handled, the Eagle was directed against a third F-111 flying at low altitude over land, and this threat too was intercepted and "destroyed". Twice more the Eagle was ordered aloft and targeted against three aircraft, and twice more the three were stopped short of their objective.

Moving to Germany, the Eagle flew three more intercepts and defeated all intruders. Following this came a North Sea combat air patrol during which two F-111s were intercepted as they approached from the north. An F-4 flying over Germany fared just as poorly. Still another mission had the same result – all targets intercepted and defeated. The final exercise pitted the Eagle, on air combat patrol at 15,000ft (4,572m), against two F-4 Phantoms flying at altitudes of between 500 and 800ft (152 and 240m). Not only did the F-15 "destroy" both intruders, but in each case it did so in a single pass.

Often, F-15s are not fired on during such exercises. They detect and destroy the threat aircraft before their pilots know the Eagles are there.

In less than an hour the strictly air-to-air Eagle can be converted for ground attack — a secondary role which the USAF demanded from the outset. By loading bombs on its three pylons, the Eagle becomes an attack aircraft capable of carrying almost 12,000lb (5,443kg) of bombs without downloading any air-to-air armament. The weapon delivery system — the same one as is used for air-to-air — is automated so that the pilot can deliver his ordnance without having to look outside the cockpit. All necessary information is on the head-up display and switches are on the stick and throttle. The Eagle is the

only USAF fighter qualified to carry and release multiple stores supersonically, and its delivery accuracy is remarkable. At 10,000ft (3,048m), for instance, an F-15 carrying conventional bombs will drop half of them on or within 65ft (19.8m) of its target. That is much better than the Phantom, which was used extensively as a fighter-bomber in South-East Asia, and slightly better on average than present day aircraft designed specifically for attack.

The airframe of the F-15 is a combination of conventional materials such as aluminium, titanium and steel coupled with proven new materials such as graphite and boron composites. Each F-15 is basically an aluminium aeroplane supplemented by titanium in high-stress,

Figs. 23 & 24 *Second development F-15B (note changed tail number) was widely used as a demonstration aircraft and had a special red, white and blue colour scheme during 1976 to mark the American Revolution Bicentennial. Note also Canadian roundel.*

Figs. 25 & 26 *Although primarily designed to excel in air-to-air combat, the F-15 has also proved extremely potent in air-to-surface missions. When carrying air-to-surface weapons, air-to-air armament is not downloaded.*

Fig. 27 F-15 has 570 sq ft (52.95m²) of access doors and panels to let the maintenance man do his job quickly.

Fig. 28 *Second F-15A (10281) in the Air Superiority Blue and dayglo finish whilst on test from Edwards AFB, California, Compare wing tips with those of production Eagles.*

fatigue and temperature-sensitive areas and by composites where both stiffness and minimum weight are required. The rugged structure provides a fatigue life four times higher than that of the Phantom, and moderate G loads can be maintained with one vertical tail, or any of the three spars in each wing completely severed. The wings are the key to the F-15's superior manoeuvra-

bility. A simple wing with no leading-edge devices was chosen after exhaustive trials and analyses of no less than 107 planforms and 800 variations, one offshoot of which was the leading-edge slat subsequently fitted on later Phantoms. Conventional and conical camber are incorporated to provide the most efficient low-drag configuration at high lift in the transonic region. Wing area

Fig. 29 *An early production F-15A carrying two 600-US gallon fuel tanks on wing pylons.*

Fig. 30 *First overseas country to receive the Eagle was Israel, who is now gradually receiving a total of 40 aircraft; one of them is shown. At the time of writing (early 1980) other customers besides the USA (729 planned) and Israel are Japan (14 plus 86 licence-built) & Saudi Arabia (60).*

is 608sq ft (56.5m²) providing the extremely low loading required.

To further increase its survivability in combat, the Eagle has many back-up systems, including dual flight controls, dual electrical systems, three hydraulic systems, back-up pumps and two generators. Redundancy is also inherent in the twin engines, and the fuel system incorporates self-sealing features and foam to inhibit fires and explosions. Yet another feature contributing to Eagle survivability is the free-fall landing gear.

Maintainability and reliability of the Eagle is a major improvement over previous fighters. The Eagle requires about 40 per cent less maintenance than the F-4E and is approximately three times more reliable. Among many features contributing to this excellent state of affairs are easy access to all components, easy engine removal and replacement (possible in less than 20 minutes), built-in test system for all avionics, numerous failure cues/indicators and eight gauges, and a 12-minute turnaround in the air-defence configuration. At Bitburg Air Base in Germany, the 36th Tactical Fighter Wing launched 322 Eagle missions in less than 24 hours, and most of the wing's 72 Eagles were ready to fly and fight again when the exercise ended. At Soesterberg Air Base in Holland, the 32nd Tactical Fighter Squadron – using just 13 F-15s per day for seven flying days – launched 439 Eagle sorties in an exercise with RAF Phantom fighters. During both exercises, the unit continued to keep fully-armed F-15s on air-defence alert at all times.

SPECIFICATION — F-15A

Powerplant: Two 25,000lb (11,340kg) thrust class Pratt & Whitney F100-100 turbofans with reheat.

Dimensions: Span 42ft 9¾in (13,05m); length 63ft 9¾in (19,45m); height 18ft 7½in (5,68m).

Weight: Empty, about 28,000lb (12,700kg); take-off, air-superiority (four Sparrow AAMs, full internal fuel) 41,500lb (18,824kg); max take-off, basic, 56,000lb (25,401kg).

Performance: Max speed (low) over 921mph (1,482km/h Mach 1·22); (high) over 1,650mph (2,660km/h Mach 2·5); initial climb, over 50,000ft/min (15,240m/min); service ceiling, 65,000ft (19,800m); range on internal fuel about 1,200 miles (1,930km); ferry range with max fuel, over 3,700 miles (5,955km).

Armament: One 20mm M61 six-barrel rapid-firing cannon in starboard wing root; four AIM-7F advanced Sparrow radar-guided AAMs on lower corners of fuselage; four AIM-9L Sidewinder heat-seeking AAMs (very effective in close combat) on two pylons under wings. Centreline pylon stressed for 4,500lb (2,041kg) for 600 US gal (2,273 litre) fuel tank, reconnaissance pod or any tactical weapon. Inner wing pylons stressed for 5,100lb (2,313kg) for any tanks or weapon. Outer wing pylons stressed for 1,000lb (454kg) for ECM pods or equivalent ordnance load. Normal external load limit 12,000lb (5,443kg).

McDONNELL DOUGLAS F-4 PHANTOM II

By Philip J. R. Moyes

Fig. 1   *A Phantom FGR2 (F-4M) of 111 Squadron, RAF Coningsby, Lincolnshire, in 1974. The aircraft is carrying underwing Sidewinder AAMs and underwing fuel tanks. In front of it are more Phantom armaments – four Sparrow AAMs and a Gatling cannon pod and ammunition.*

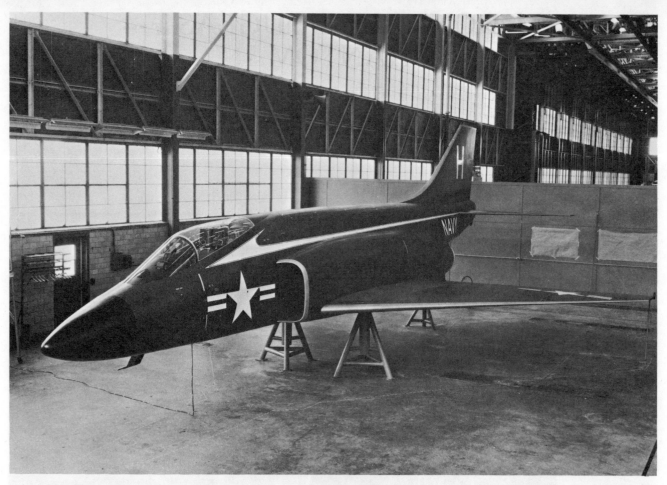

Fig. 2 *McDonnell's company-financed mock-up of the Phantom-to-be, then identified as the F3H-G. Note particularly the single cockpit, the unbroken lines of the wing, and the undrooped tail.* Fig. 3 *The mock-up after reconfiguration into the F4H-1, with revised inlets, second cockpit, and drooped tailplane. Sparrow missiles were to be launched from extendable rails.*

Fig. 4 *The Royal Australian Air Force "borrowed" 24 F-4E Phantoms from the USAF whilst awaiting deliveries of General Dynamics F-111Cs. The Phantoms were delivered from St Louis in late 1970 and 23 of them were eventually returned to the USAF.*

The McDonnell Douglas F-4 Phantom II is among the most versatile and popular fighter aircraft of all time. It is also the most-produced supersonic jet fighter in the free world, with a total of some 5,100 delivered by McDonnell Douglas before production ended in 1979; in addition, Japan has built 156 under licence. Fifteen main distinct models have been developed and The Fabulous Phantom, as it has so deservedly been called, has flown with the air arms of 11 nations − The USA, Great Britain, Australia, Egypt, Federal Germany, Greece, Iran, Japan, South Korea, Spain and Turkey; and it has achieved more than 277 air-to-air victories in combat.

Preliminary design of what was to become the Phantom II was begun in the summer of 1953, by which time McDonnell, of St Louis, Missouri, had built more than 1,000 carrier-based jet aircraft − the FH-1 Phantom (the US Navy's first jet-powered carrier-based plane), the F2H Banshee, and the F3H Demon. The still fairly young firm had recently lost a new carrier-based supersonic day fighter competition − the winner having been the Chance Vought Crusader − but, determined to press on in its main sphere of interest, it embarked on a new project to meet anticipated future needs of the Navy. Unofficially known as the F3H-G/H, this was a large single-seater with four internal 20mm cannon, provision in the nose for a relatively large radar, and no fewer than 11 external pylons for stores. Powered by two Wright J65 turbojets (licence-built Armstrong Siddeley Sapphires) it was considered capable of attaining Mach 1.5 at high altitude and in general appearance it was not unlike the eventual Phantom II, although the wing and tailplane were flat.

Navy interest in a privately-financed full-scale mock-up led to McDonnell being sent a letter of intent in October 1954 for two prototypes of what officially became designated the AH-1, the "A" indicating that the aircraft was seen as an attack bomber rather than a fighter. Among several changes stipulated by the Navy at this time was a switch from Wright J65 engines to more powerful General Electric J79s.

Several months work on the project was scrapped early in 1955 when the Navy requested fundamental changes to make the AH-1's role that of a missile-armed long-range all-weather interceptor. Accordingly, the designation was changed to F4H-1 and McDonnell

23

Fig. 5 *The prototype F4H-1 (US Navy Bureau number 142259) pictured at Lambert-St Louis Municipal Airport where it first flew on 27 May 1958.*

reconfigured the design by removing the four cannon, changing the fire-control system to be compatible with air-to-air missiles, and deleting all external armament stations except one at the centreline for a large auxiliary fuel tank. At this time, the Raytheon Sparrow AAM was in the development phase, and the aircraft was configured to carry four, semi-submerged in the bottom of the fuselage – the first such installation of missiles in a fighter. The J79 engines that were to power the aircraft,

plus other features, would make it the Navy's first Mach 2-plus carrier-based aircraft. During this period, the Navy was undecided on a single or two-seat aircraft, but McDonnell prepared configurations of both and the Navy chose the two-seat version, this subsequently proving to be the most significant change of all and perhaps the major factor in the longevity of the Phantom.

The original Navy contract for two YAH-1s was changed to one for 23 F4H-1 development aircraft, and

Fig. 6 *Pair of bomb-laden F-4Bs of VMFA-513, USMC.*

Fig. 7 *Rip-roaring take-off study of an RAAF F-4E from RAAF base Amberley, Queensland. The Phantom's fast climb rate makes it one of the most deadly strike aircraft in the world today.*

as McDonnell's earlier FH-1 Phantom was no longer in service, the new type was named Phantom II. The F4H-1 took to the air on 27 May 1958 from Lambert-St Louis Municipal Airport in the hands of McDonnell's chief test pilot, Robert C. Little. Problems during the type's flight test programme were few and performance phenomenal. Following competitive evaluation against the Chance Vought F8U-3 Crusader III, the F4H-1 was chosen as new standard US Navy equipment in

December 1958, and preparations for full-scale production began. In February 1960, carrier suitability trials were conducted aboard USS *Independence,* and on 29 December that year the Phantom joined the fleet when the first production aircraft – No 28 – was delivered to squadron VF-121 at Naval Air Station Miramar, California, which was to equip for transition training.

The initial production batch of Phantoms (24 aircraft, Nos 24 to 47 inclusive) were followed by 696

Fig. 8 *McDonnell's original Phantom. First of two XFD-1s (one is shown) first flew in January 1945 and production of the type as the FD-1 totalled just 60.*

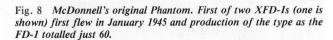

25

Fig. 9 Only non-US operator of F-4Cs has been the Spanish Air Force which received 36 from the USAF in 1971-72. Spain later received a few RF-4Cs.

26

Fig. 10 *Carrier suitability trials were conducted with the sixth F4H-1 (Bu no 143391) aboard the USS* **Independence** *beginning 15 February 1960.*

Fig. 11 *The third F4H-1 (Bu no 143388) refuels in flight from a Douglas A3D-2 Skywarrior.*

definitive F4H-1s with improvements in the engine and fire-control system, a high canopy, and a longer-range radar. All the first 47 F4H-1s were redesignated F4H-1F in March 1961, and it was on the 25th of that month that the first of the improved production aircraft flew. Deliveries of the latter to the Navy began in June 1961 and the first operational Phantom squadrons, VF-74 and VF-114, started to receive the type the following month. Another noteworthy milestone in the Phantom's maritime career came on 29 June 1972 when a F4H-1 was delivered to a US Marine Corps squadron,

VMF(AW)-314.

Competitive evaluation tests held in 1961 showed that the Phantom outperformed all the USAF's existing fighters by a wide margin, with the result that in March 1962 the USAF decided to adopt it – an unprecedented move since the service had never before purchased a plane primarily designed for carrier operations. For a short time, the initial USAF versions were designated F-110A and RF-110A, the latter being a fighter-reconnaissance aircraft. However, when in September 1962 the US services adopted a new unified designation

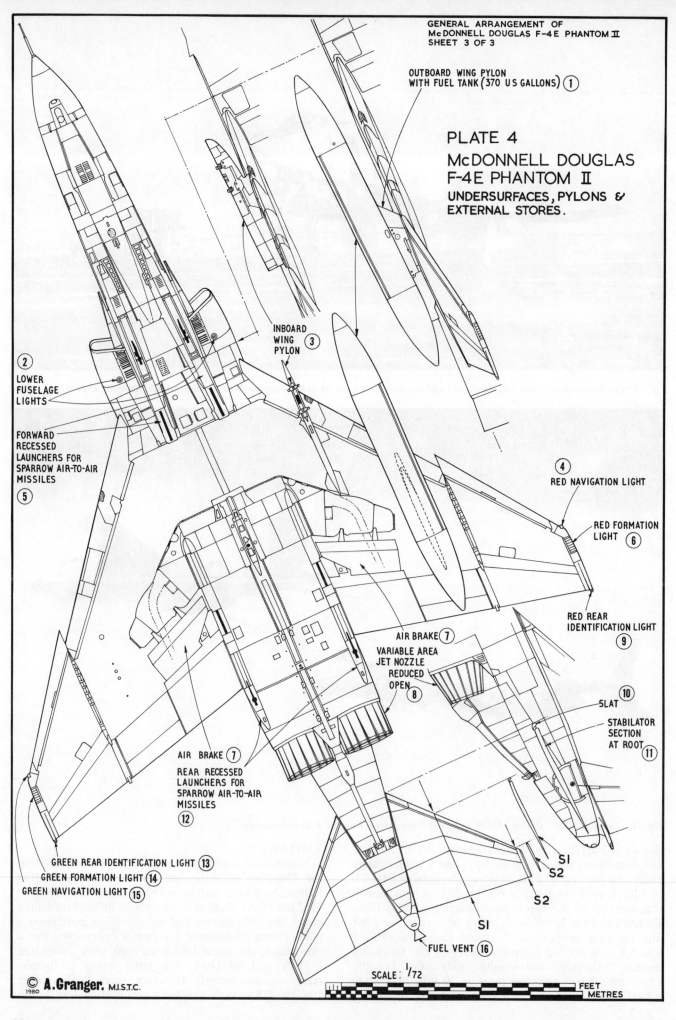

OUTBOARD WING PYLON
WITH FUEL TANK (370 US GALLONS) ①

PLATE 4
McDONNELL DOUGLAS
F-4E PHANTOM II
UNDERSURFACES, PYLONS &
EXTERNAL STORES.

INBOARD
WING
PYLON ③

② LOWER
FUSELAGE
LIGHTS

FORWARD
RECESSED
LAUNCHERS FOR
SPARROW AIR-TO-AIR
MISSILES
⑤

④
RED NAVIGATION LIGHT

RED FORMATION
LIGHT
⑥

RED REAR
IDENTIFICATION LIGHT
⑨

AIR BRAKE ⑦

VARIABLE AREA
JET NOZZLE
REDUCED
OPEN
⑧

⑩
SLAT

STABILATOR
SECTION
AT ROOT
⑪

AIR BRAKE ⑦

REAR RECESSED
LAUNCHERS FOR
SPARROW AIR-TO-AIR
MISSILES
⑫

S1
S2

S2

S1

GREEN REAR IDENTIFICATION LIGHT ⑬
GREEN FORMATION LIGHT ⑭
GREEN NAVIGATION LIGHT ⑮

FUEL VENT ⑯

SCALE: 1/72

FEET
METRES

RESEARCH: A. GRANGER © 1980
ARTWORK: ROY MILLS

PLATE 1

McDONNELL DOUGLAS
F-4E PHANTOM
67-266 OF 36th TFW
BITBURG AB 1975

SCALE 1/144.

DETAIL OF FIN MARKINGS   SCALE 1/72   ①

DETAIL OF
NATIONAL
INSIGNIA
SCALE 1/72.
②

29

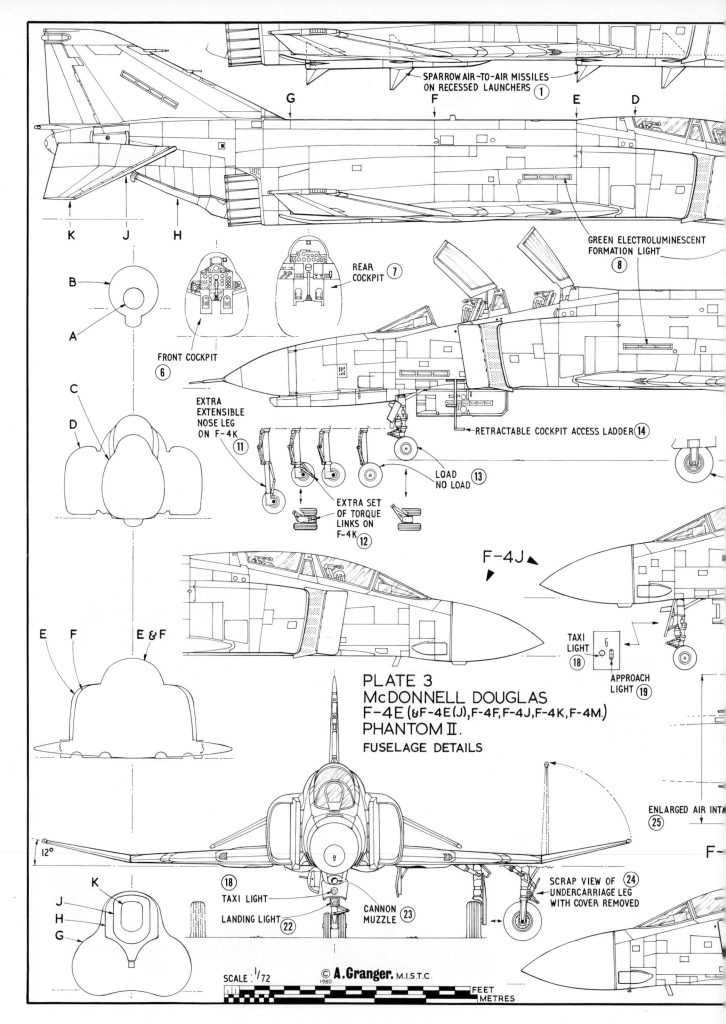

SPARROW AIR-TO-AIR MISSILES
ON RECESSED LAUNCHERS (1)

G   F   E   D

K   J   H

GREEN ELECTROLUMINESCENT
FORMATION LIGHT (8)

B

A

REAR COCKPIT (7)

C

D

FRONT COCKPIT (6)

EXTRA EXTENSIBLE NOSE LEG ON F-4K (11)

RETRACTABLE COCKPIT ACCESS LADDER (14)

LOAD NO LOAD (13)

EXTRA SET OF TORQUE LINKS ON F-4K (12)

F-4J ▶

E   F   E & F

TAXI LIGHT (18)

APPROACH LIGHT (19)

PLATE 3
McDONNELL DOUGLAS
F-4E (&F-4E(J), F-4F, F-4J, F-4K, F-4M.)
PHANTOM II.
FUSELAGE DETAILS

ENLARGED AIR INTA... (25)

12°

K

J

H

G

(18) TAXI LIGHT

LANDING LIGHT (22)

CANNON MUZZLE (23)

SCRAP VIEW OF (24)
UNDERCARRIAGE LEG
WITH COVER REMOVED

SCALE ¹/₇₂

© A. Granger. M.I.S.T.C.
1980

FEET
METRES

30

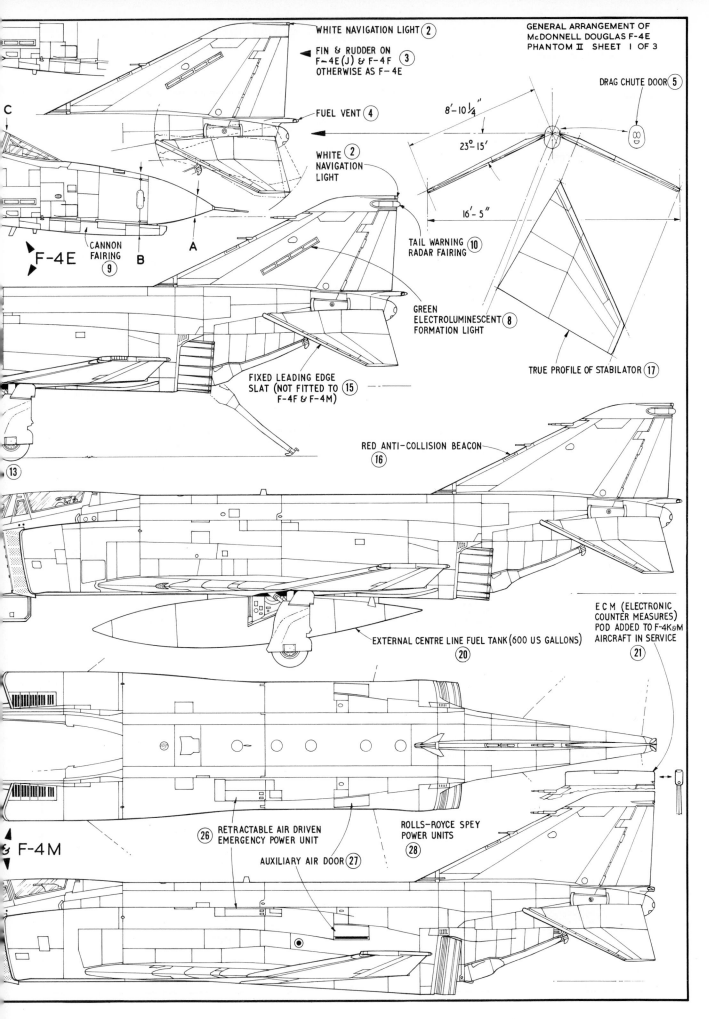

WHITE NAVIGATION LIGHT ②

FIN & RUDDER ON
F-4E(J) & F-4F ③
OTHERWISE AS F-4E

FUEL VENT ④

DRAG CHUTE DOOR ⑤

8'-10¼"

23°-15'

16'-5"

WHITE
NAVIGATION ②
LIGHT

C

F-4E

CANNON
FAIRING ⑨

B   A

TAIL WARNING
RADAR FAIRING ⑩

GREEN
ELECTROLUMINESCENT ⑧
FORMATION LIGHT

TRUE PROFILE OF STABILATOR ⑰

FIXED LEADING EDGE
SLAT (NOT FITTED TO ⑮
F-4F & F-4M)

RED ANTI-COLLISION BEACON
⑯

⑬

EXTERNAL CENTRE LINE FUEL TANK (600 US GALLONS)
⑳

ECM (ELECTRONIC
COUNTER MEASURES)
POD ADDED TO F-4K&M
AIRCRAFT IN SERVICE
㉑

& F-4M

RETRACTABLE AIR DRIVEN
㉖ EMERGENCY POWER UNIT

AUXILIARY AIR DOOR ㉗

ROLLS-ROYCE SPEY
POWER UNITS
㉘

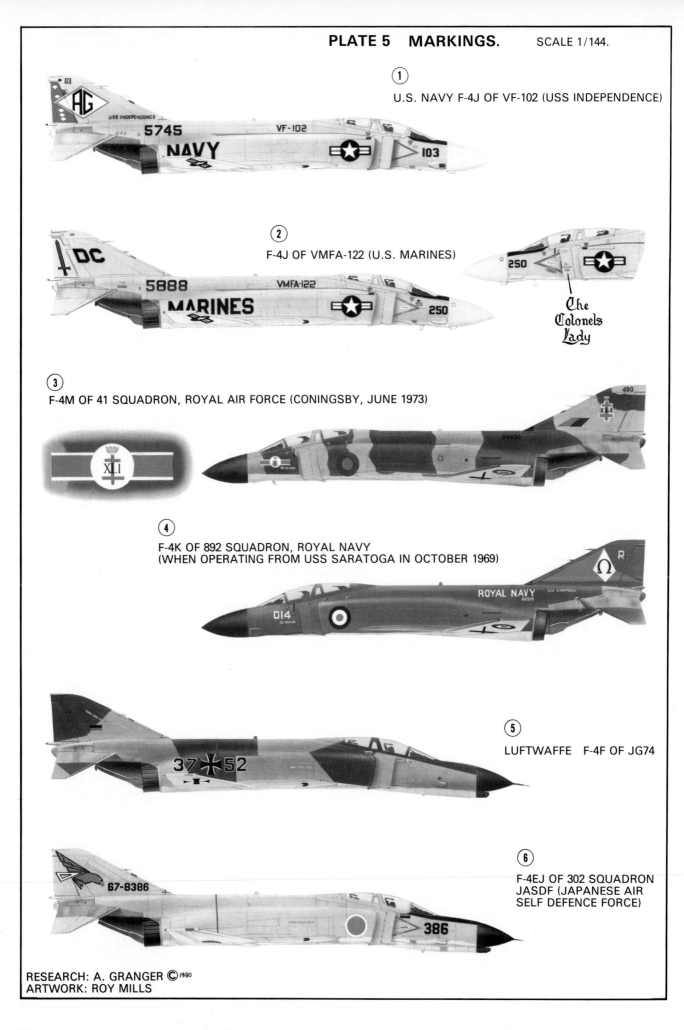

PLATE 5 MARKINGS.   SCALE 1/144.

① U.S. NAVY F-4J OF VF-102 (USS INDEPENDENCE)

② F-4J OF VMFA-122 (U.S. MARINES)

The Colonels Lady

③ F-4M OF 41 SQUADRON, ROYAL AIR FORCE (CONINGSBY, JUNE 1973)

④ F-4K OF 892 SQUADRON, ROYAL NAVY
(WHEN OPERATING FROM USS SARATOGA IN OCTOBER 1969)

⑤ LUFTWAFFE   F-4F OF JG74

⑥ F-4EJ OF 302 SQUADRON
JASDF (JAPANESE AIR
SELF DEFENCE FORCE)

RESEARCH: A. GRANGER ©1980
ARTWORK: ROY MILLS

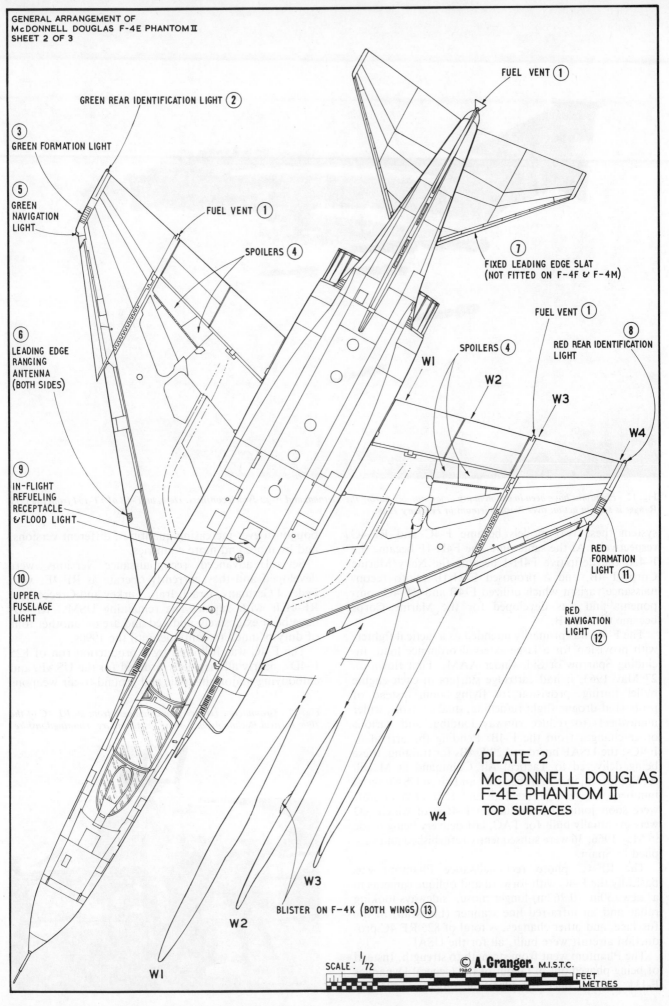

FUEL VENT ①

GREEN REAR IDENTIFICATION LIGHT ②

③ GREEN FORMATION LIGHT

⑤ GREEN NAVIGATION LIGHT

FUEL VENT ①

SPOILERS ④

⑦ FIXED LEADING EDGE SLAT (NOT FITTED ON F-4F & F-4M)

⑥ LEADING EDGE RANGING ANTENNA (BOTH SIDES)

FUEL VENT ①

SPOILERS ④

W1

W2

W3

W4

⑧ RED REAR IDENTIFICATION LIGHT

⑨ IN-FLIGHT REFUELING RECEPTACLE & FLOOD LIGHT

⑩ UPPER FUSELAGE LIGHT

RED FORMATION LIGHT ⑪

RED NAVIGATION LIGHT ⑫

PLATE 2
McDONNELL DOUGLAS
F-4E PHANTOM II
TOP SURFACES

W4

W3

W2

W1

BLISTER ON F-4K (BOTH WINGS) ⑬

SCALE: 1/72

© A.Granger. M.I.S.T.C.
1980

FEET
METRES

33

Fig. 12 *Phantoms have been in action many times, notably during the Vietnam and Arab-Israeli conflicts. Here, an F-4B of VF-154 from the USS* **Ranger** *is seen in action over North Vietnam in February 1968.*

system these two models became F-4C and RF-4C respectively. At the same time, the F4H-1F became the F-4A, the definitive F4H-1 became the Navy/Marine Corps F-4B, and a proposed F4H-1P photo reconnaissance variant which utilized F-4B and RF-4C components and was developed for the Marine Corps became the RF-4B.

The F-4C was primarily intended as a tactical fighter, with provision for a large external ordnance load, including Sparrow or Sidewinder AAMs. First flown on 27 May 1963, it had cartridge starters in each engine bullet fairing, provision for flying-boom instead of probe-and-drogue flight refuelling, dual controls, wider mainwheels to reduce runway loading, and various other changes from the F-4B. Pending the arrival of F-4Cs, the USAF borrowed 29 F-4Bs for training, these being delivered to Tactical Air Command at McDill AFB, Florida, in November 1963 and given USAF serial numbers. However, these 12th and 15th TFW aircraft were soon joined by production F-4Cs, of which 583 were eventually built for TAC, last delivery being made in May 1966; 36 were subsequently refurbished and supplied to Spain.

The RF-4C photo reconnaissance Phantom was basically the F-4C with forward and oblique cameras in a new 30in (0.762m)-longer nose, sideways-looking radar and an infra-red line scanner (Linescan) in the fuselage, and other changes. A total of 825 RF-4C production aircraft were built, all for the USAF.

The Phantom went from strength to strength. Instead of being phased out in favour of the General Dynamics F-111, as was once the plan, the older aircraft was

bought in ever-increasing quantities, different versions, and by more and more countries.

Several advanced reconnaissance versions were developed and they currently operate as RF-4Es with Federal Germany, Israel, Iran, Turkey and Greece, and RF-4EJs with Japan. The remaining USMC RF-4Bs have been extensively updated and are on another tour of duty planned to continue until the 1990s.

The F-4C was followed by a production run of 825 F-4Ds, nearly all originally ordered for the USAF, and embodying major air-to-air and ground-to-air weapons

Fig. 13 *Groundcrew remove film containers from an RF-4C of the 10th Tactical Reconnaissance Wing at Alconbury, Huntingdonshire.*

delivery improvements. Pylon-mounted ordnance of the D could include Maverick and Falcon missiles or laser-guided "smart" bombs. Two foreign recipients of F-4Ds were Iran, who purchased 32, and the Republic of Korea, whose 36 machines were diverted from the USAF orders for a total of 793 D-models.

June 1967 saw Phantom output reach a peak monthly rate of 72 aircraft. It also saw the first flight of the production model F-4E (YF-4E prototype flew August 1965) which proved to be the major Phantom production model with 1,389 delivered eventually. Originally developed for the Air Force, the E came in a number of versions, each adapted to the particular user, and they included improved radar, an improved intertial navigation system, and a permanent installation of an M61 rotary-barrel 20mm cannon under the nose. Late production E models introduced leading-edge slots on the all-moving tailplane and automatic manoeuvring slats on the outer wing leading edge in place of blown flaps. These slats, which were spin-off from F-15 Eagle wing development (but not used on that fighter) were fitted to other F-4Es retrospectively.

The F-4F (175 assembled by McDonnell Douglas from assemblies built in Germany) was one of the F-4E based versions just referred to and was developed for the Luftwaffe, while the designation F-4G was first given to 12 F-4Bs modified for the US Navy to test automatic carrier landing systems. (The F-4G designation was subsequently re-used, of which more anon).

To succeed the F-4B as the US Navy's and US Marine Corps' standard production model came the F-4J (prototype flown June 1965, first production flight May 1966, and a total of 522 delivered by January 1972) featuring such improvements as new radar, extra fuel tankage, slotted tailplane, electronic countermeasures (ECM), larger mainwheels as per the F-4E, and a general beef-up.

Fig. 14 *Maverick missile with an imaging infrared (IR) seeker, mounted on a Phantom, receives final checkout before being flown to Europe for captive flight tests — a photo released in January 1978.*

In 1966, the F-4K, utilizing Rolls-Royce Spey turbofan engines, was developed for the Royal Navy of Great Britain — first foreign country to order the Phantom — and a year later the F-4M was developed for the Royal Air Force. A total of 170 production examples of these two versions were built and they incorporated British-specified equipment and design features.

Fig. 15 *Late production F-4Es and 'Fs introduced leading edge slots on the all-moving tailplane and automatic manoeuvring slats on the outer wing leading edge in place of blown flaps. These slats were retrofitted by the USAF on earlier examples of the F-4E.*

Fig. 16 Close-up of the leading edge manoeuvring slats which further improve the Phantom's famous combat agility. The extendable slats provide higher buffet-free lift than earlier versions of the Phantom, while reducing drag at high angles of attack.

Fig. 17   An F-4B of VF-14 is prepared for launching from the attack carrier USS FD Roosevelt steaming in the Gulf of Tonkin during the Vietnam War.

37

Fig. 18 *The Republic of Korea has been supplied with F-4Ds and 'Es, one of which latter is shown.*   Fig. 19 *The Hellenic Air Force began obtaining F-4Es (example shown) in 1974, and later added the RF-4E to its inventory.*

Fig. 20 *Iran began acquiring the Phantom by ordering F-4Ds in 1966. Deliveries began in September 1968 and continued through late 1969. Iran has also been supplied with some RF-4Es.*

Short Brothers & Harland. As a result of agreements between the US government and the Federal Republic of Germany, the German aerospace firms Messerschmitt, Dornier, and VFW-Fokker, produced over 9,200 major assemblies worth more than $130 million to be used in Phantom aircraft delivered world-wide.

Early in production, as much as 55 per cent of the airframe by weight was manufactured by other major US aircraft contractors and 4,200 other, smaller concerns have provided bits and pieces. Now, McDonnell Douglas has helped rebuild the Phantom. A large number of USAF F-4Es are currently being converted to F-4G Wild Weasels, highly sophisticated ECM aircraft with provision to carry offensive missiles. At the time of writing, the US Navy, with McDonnell Douglas' help, is in the process of updating the F-4J to the F-4S to incorporate, among other things, the leading edge manoeuvering slats. A total of 302 of these aircraft will be updated and returned to the inventory for use until the 1990s – a follow-up to 178 F-4Bs which were updated (but not given wing slats) during 1972-73 and redesignated F-4N.

Fig. 21 For five years from 1969 the F-4E was the mount of the famous **Thunderbirds** *air demonstration squadron of the USAF, and during that time the Phantoms' exciting close-formation aerobatics represented American air power and friendship all over the free world.*

As already mentioned, more than 5,100 Phantoms have been delivered by McDonnell Douglas to US forces and America's allies, an additional 156 Phantoms having been built in Japan under licence. The latter are F-4EJs, (basically F-4Es) and were in fact assembled/built by Mitsubishi after two pattern aircraft had been supplied by McDonnell Douglas. These international programmes created nearly $5 billion in balance-of-payments credit and have effected an over $3.25 billion reduction in the cost of the Phantom to the US government. These sales also created over 250,000 man-years of US industry employment.

Many companies throughout the world have participated and shared in the Phantom's success, for the Phantom has never been a one-company project. Forty-five per cent of the dollar value of the K and M programme was produced in the United Kingdom. The major airframe contractors were British Aerospace and

SPECIFICATION — F-4E Phantom II

Powerplant: Two General Electric J79-GE-17 turbojets each with a normal continuous rating of 11,110lb (5044kg) thrust, and a maximum rating with reheat of 17,900lb (8127kg) thrust.

Dimensions: Span 38ft 4in (11,68m); span folded 27ft 6in (8,38m); length 63ft 0in (19,20m); height 16ft 5in (5,00m).

Weight: Empty 30,328lb (13,770kg); maximum loaded 61,795lb (28,055kg). Performance: Max speed Mach 2.7 (1,432mph/2304km/h); maximum rate of climb (clean) 49,800ft/minimum (253m/sec); service ceiling (clean) 58,750ft (17,907m).

Armament: One General Electric M61A1 multi-barrel 20mm rotary cannon under forward fuselage with 640 rounds; four/six AIM-7E Sparrow AAMs plus four AIM-D Sidewinder AAMs; up to 16,000lb (7257 kg) of conventional or nuclear stores.

Fig. 22 For five seasons from 1969 the US Navy's **Blue Angels** *flight demonstration team thrilled millions worldwide with their exhibitions of precision flying using the F-4B as their mount.*

Fig. 23   Royal Navy Phantom FG1 (F-4K) XT872 of 892 Squadron
lands aboard the USS Independence during a NATO exercise in
November 1975. Phantoms have since been withdrawn from the Royal
Navy.

Fig. 24 · One latter-day development in the Phantom programme was the conversion of several USN
F-4Bs into QF-4B drones for use by the Naval Missile Center at Point Mugu, California.

THE LOCKHEED F-104 STARFIGHTER

By Philip J. R. Moyes

Fig. 1 *The first XF-104 in flight.*

Fig. 2 *The second YF-104 appeared at the marque's press début in April 1956 but had its air intakes blanked off for security reasons.*

Dubbed "the missile with a man in it", the radical Lockheed F-104 Starfighter was the first operational combat aeroplane capable of sustaining Mach 2 speeds and the first plane to hold both speed and altitude records simultaneously.

Fig. 3 *Another view of the second YF-104A taken at the press début at Palmdale. Note the extremely narrow-track undercarriage.*

In the 1960s, it was one of the most widely-used fighters in the world. It has also been the centre of more controversy than any other aircraft to date, because of its very high accident rate — at least in German service; yet, all things considered, it undeniably remains one of the most remarkable aircraft of all time.

The Starfighter story began in 1951 when USAF experience in Korea with first-generation jet fighters spotlighted the need for a much lighter and faster combat plane. A Lockheed team led by the firm's chief engineer, Clarence L. "Kelly" Johnson and working at top pressure in the famous "Skunk Works" at Burbank, California — a factory so-called because of the striking black and white mat in its entrance lobby — started to scheme a series of light fighter projects. Design work on what eventually became the F-104 began in November 1952, a USAF contract for two prototypes was placed in March 1953, and eleven months later, on 7 February 1954, the first XF-104A (53-7786) flew, in the hands of Lockheed's chief experimental test pilot, Tony LeVier. Both prototypes had a 10,000lb (4536kg) thrust afterburning Wright J-65 engine based

on the British Armstrong Siddeley Sapphire.

So secret was the project that the press were not shown the new combat plane that was about twice as fast as any previous operational aircraft until April 1956 when Lockheed and the USAF staged a Hollywood-style preview at the Palmdale jet centre featuring the second YF-104A evaluation machine (55-2956). What spectators saw as a huge curtain parted in the hangar was a pencil-thin fuselage. They saw an unswept, extremely thin wing whose leading edge was almost razor sharp; altogether flipper-like it spanned an unbelievably short 21ft 11in (6680mm) and had an anhedral angle of 10 degrees. They saw a T-shaped "flying tail". And they saw an afterburner-equipped General Electric J-79 engine capable of delivering more thrust per pound of weight than any other engine yet developed.

As part of its main armament the Starfighter incorporated the then also new M-61 Vulcan cannon, with a series of revolving barrels like the old Gatling gun, that could spew 20mm shells at a rate of 6,000 per minute — that's 100 per second — because there might be time for only one quick pass at a supersonic target.

43

Fig. 4   *The two XF-104s together in flight. The second machine shows off the marque's dagger-like plan-view to advantage.*

Fig. 5 *Close-up of a two-seat F-104B showing the razor-thin wing and the highly ingenious main undercarriage.*

Because the Starfighter's wings were so thin — thickness/chord ratio was only 3.4 per cent — they were of almost "solid" construction. This meant that the wheels, internal fuel and the Vulcan cannon had to be housed in the fuselage, and as regards the undercarriage in particular, Kelly Johnson's Skunk Works team achieved miracles in designing main legs that were hinged on oblique axes, so that the wheels lay flush within the fuselage skin when retracted.

Fifteen YF-104As were built, and these had shock-

control cones on the air intakes to position the supersonic shock waves inside the duct, forward (instead of rearward) retracting nose undercarriage, and a lengthened fuselage to accommodate more fuel. These features were retained in the 153 F-104A production aircraft, the first of which flew on 17 February 1956, but before deliveries could begin the Starfighter was plagued by unexpected and very severe development problems, including a tendency to super-stall, or in other words to stabilise in a stalled attitude from which recovery is impossible. This was not completely cured until April 1957. Another very protracted programme was that which was necessary to eliminate the tendency

Figs. 6 & 7 *An F-104A with Sidewinder AAMs at the wing tips.*

of the wing-tip fuel tanks to slam into the fuselage upon being jettisoned.

The F-104A was finally released for service in January 1958, when deliveries were made to the 83rd Fighter Intercepter Wing, Air Defense Command, at Hamilton AFB, California, but soon afterwards the aircraft were grounded due to serious engine troubles. The problems were cured by the substitution of an improved J79 engine, and the A model was joined in Air Defense Command service by the tandem two-seat F-104B tactical fighter/trainer. A total of 26 B models were built,

the prototype making its first flight on 7 February 1956.

As the marque continued to suffer a high accident rate and also because of its poor range and lack of all-weather capability, the A and B models were withdrawn from Air Defense Command by 1960, 24 of them being converted in 1960 and 1961 to remotely-controlled recoverable target drones designated QF-104. After a spell with the National Guard, some F-104As and Bs returned to service with Air Defense Command early in 1963, as a result of the Cuban crisis, and were joined by some F-104Cs transferred from Tactical Air Command.

47

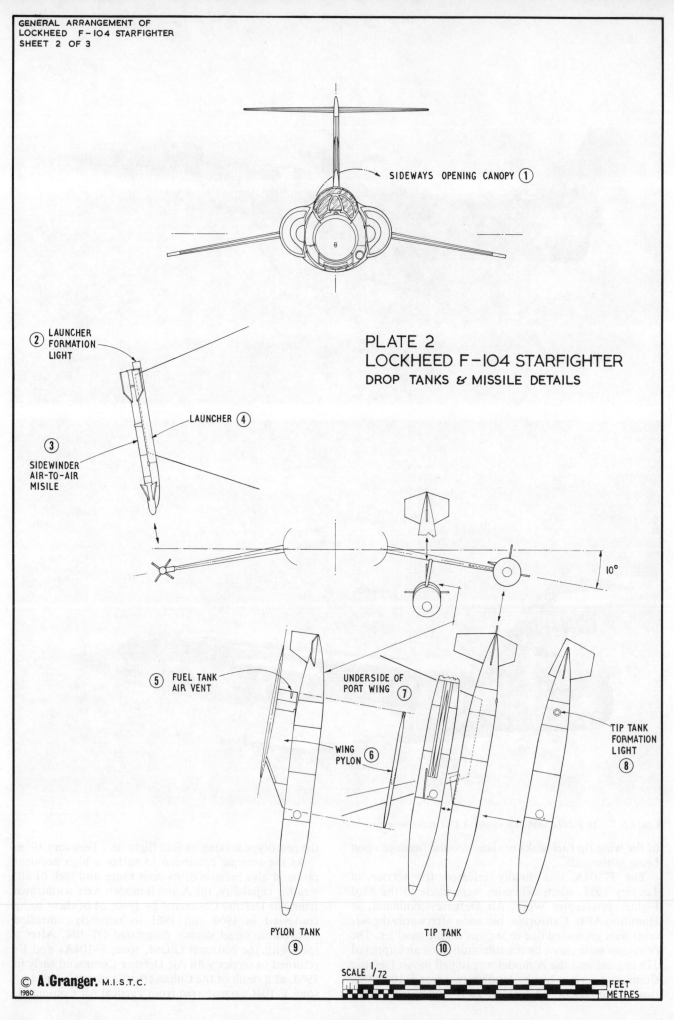

SIDEWAYS OPENING CANOPY (1)

(2) LAUNCHER
FORMATION
LIGHT

LAUNCHER (4)

(3)
SIDEWINDER
AIR-TO-AIR
MISILE

PLATE 2
LOCKHEED F-104 STARFIGHTER
DROP TANKS & MISSILE DETAILS

10°

(5) FUEL TANK
AIR VENT

UNDERSIDE OF
PORT WING (7)

TIP TANK
FORMATION
LIGHT
(8)

WING
PYLON (6)

PYLON TANK
(9)

TIP TANK
(10)

SCALE 1/72

FEET
METRES

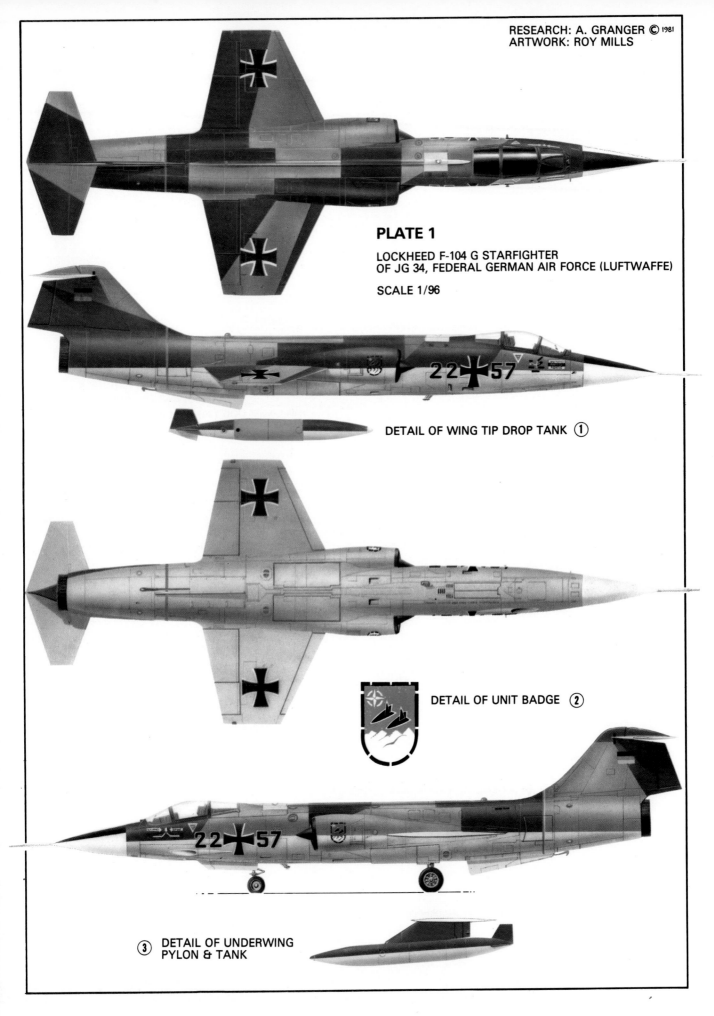

PLATE 1

LOCKHEED F-104 G STARFIGHTER
OF JG 34, FEDERAL GERMAN AIR FORCE (LUFTWAFFE)

SCALE 1/96

DETAIL OF WING TIP DROP TANK ①

DETAIL OF UNIT BADGE ②

③ DETAIL OF UNDERWING
PYLON & TANK

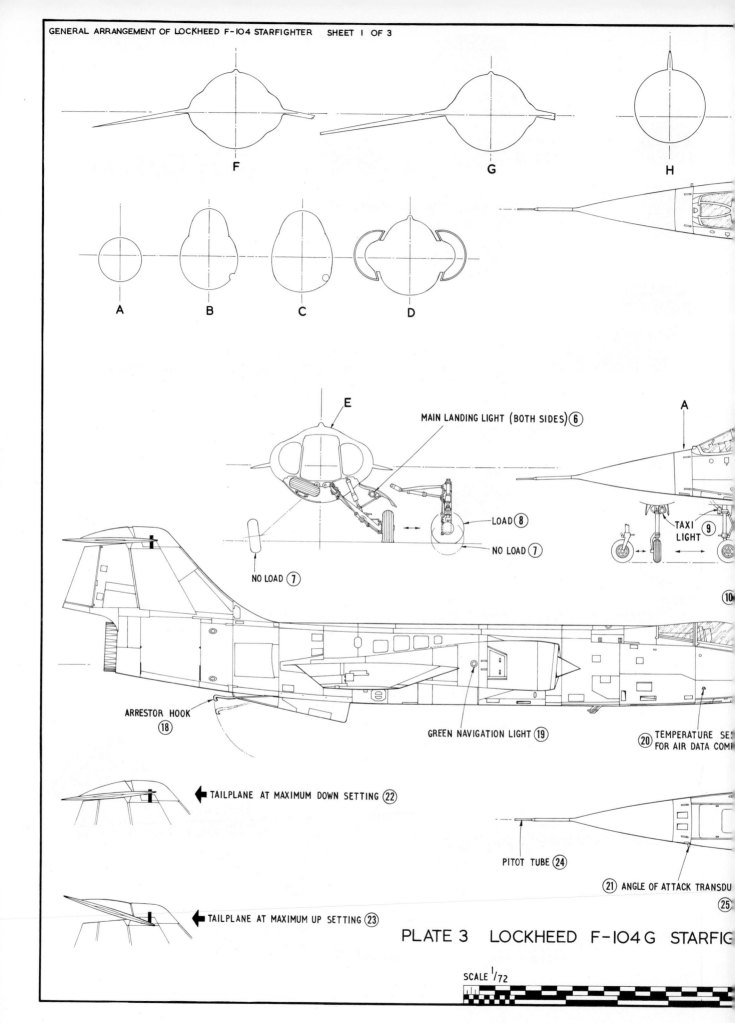

F

G

H

A

B

C

D

E

MAIN LANDING LIGHT (BOTH SIDES) ⑥

A

NO LOAD ⑦

LOAD ⑧

NO LOAD ⑦

TAXI LIGHT ⑨

ARRESTOR HOOK ⑱

GREEN NAVIGATION LIGHT ⑲

TEMPERATURE SE⸱ FOR AIR DATA COM⸱ ⑳

TAILPLANE AT MAXIMUM DOWN SETTING ㉒

TAILPLANE AT MAXIMUM UP SETTING ㉓

PITOT TUBE ㉔

㉑ ANGLE OF ATTACK TRANSDU⸱

㉕

PLATE 3   LOCKHEED F-IO4G STARFIG⸱

SCALE ¹/₇₂

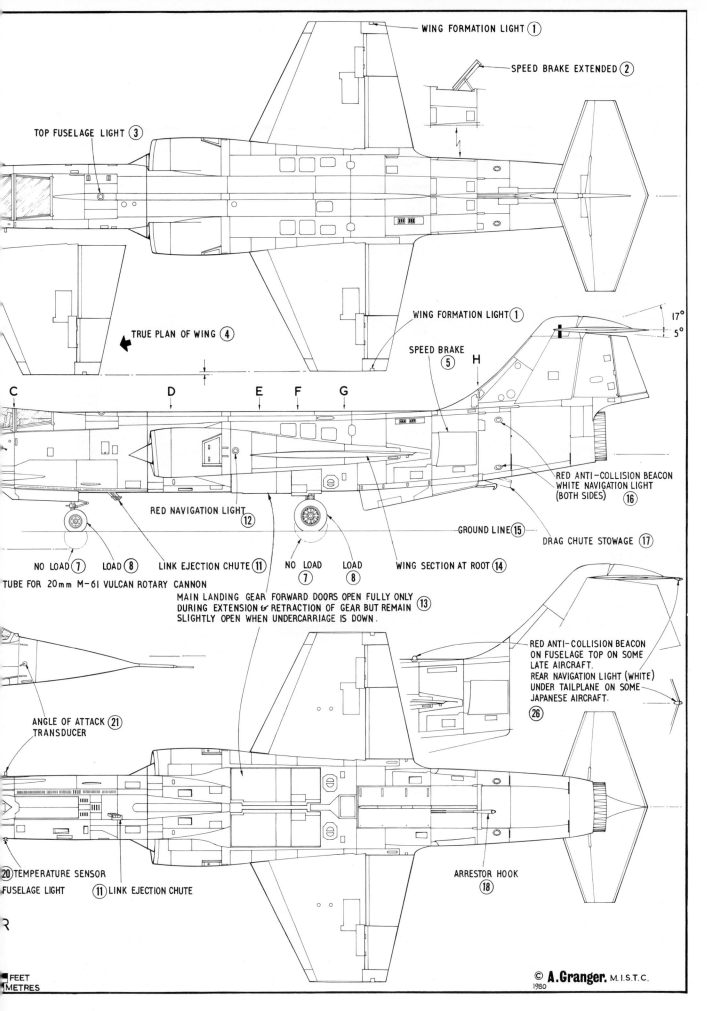

WING FORMATION LIGHT ①

SPEED BRAKE EXTENDED ②

TOP FUSELAGE LIGHT ③

TRUE PLAN OF WING ④

WING FORMATION LIGHT ①

17°
5°

SPEED BRAKE
⑤

H

C

D E F G

RED ANTI-COLLISION BEACON
WHITE NAVIGATION LIGHT
(BOTH SIDES)
⑯

RED NAVIGATION LIGHT
⑫

GROUND LINE ⑮

DRAG CHUTE STOWAGE ⑰

NO LOAD ⑦   LOAD ⑧   LINK EJECTION CHUTE ⑪   NO LOAD ⑦   LOAD ⑧   WING SECTION AT ROOT ⑭

TUBE FOR 20mm M-61 VULCAN ROTARY CANNON

MAIN LANDING GEAR FORWARD DOORS OPEN FULLY ONLY
DURING EXTENSION & RETRACTION OF GEAR BUT REMAIN   ⑬
SLIGHTLY OPEN WHEN UNDERCARRIAGE IS DOWN.

RED ANTI-COLLISION BEACON
ON FUSELAGE TOP ON SOME
LATE AIRCRAFT.
REAR NAVIGATION LIGHT (WHITE)
UNDER TAILPLANE ON SOME
JAPANESE AIRCRAFT.
㉖

ANGLE OF ATTACK ㉑
TRANSDUCER

⑳ TEMPERATURE SENSOR
FUSELAGE LIGHT   ⑪ LINK EJECTION CHUTE

ARRESTOR HOOK
⑱

R

FEET
METRES

© A.Granger. M.I.S.T.C.
1980

51

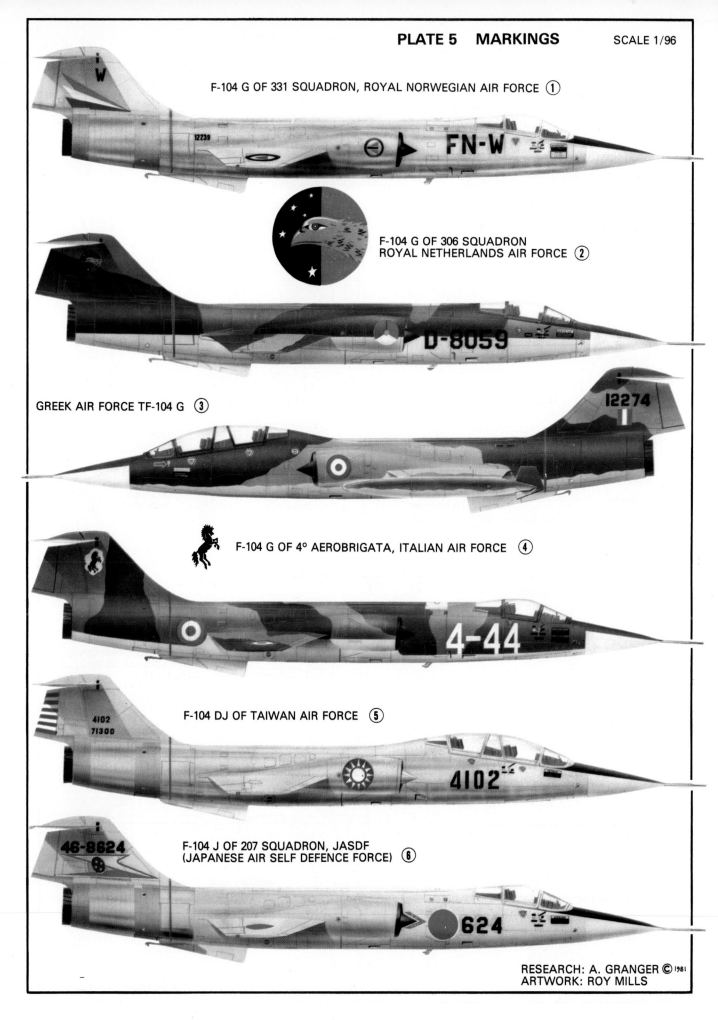

PLATE 5 MARKINGS

SCALE 1/96

F-104 G OF 331 SQUADRON, ROYAL NORWEGIAN AIR FORCE ①

F-104 G OF 306 SQUADRON
ROYAL NETHERLANDS AIR FORCE ②

GREEK AIR FORCE TF-104 G ③

F-104 G OF 4° AEROBRIGATA, ITALIAN AIR FORCE ④

F-104 DJ OF TAIWAN AIR FORCE ⑤

F-104 J OF 207 SQUADRON, JASDF
(JAPANESE AIR SELF DEFENCE FORCE) ⑥

RESEARCH: A. GRANGER © 1981
ARTWORK: ROY MILLS

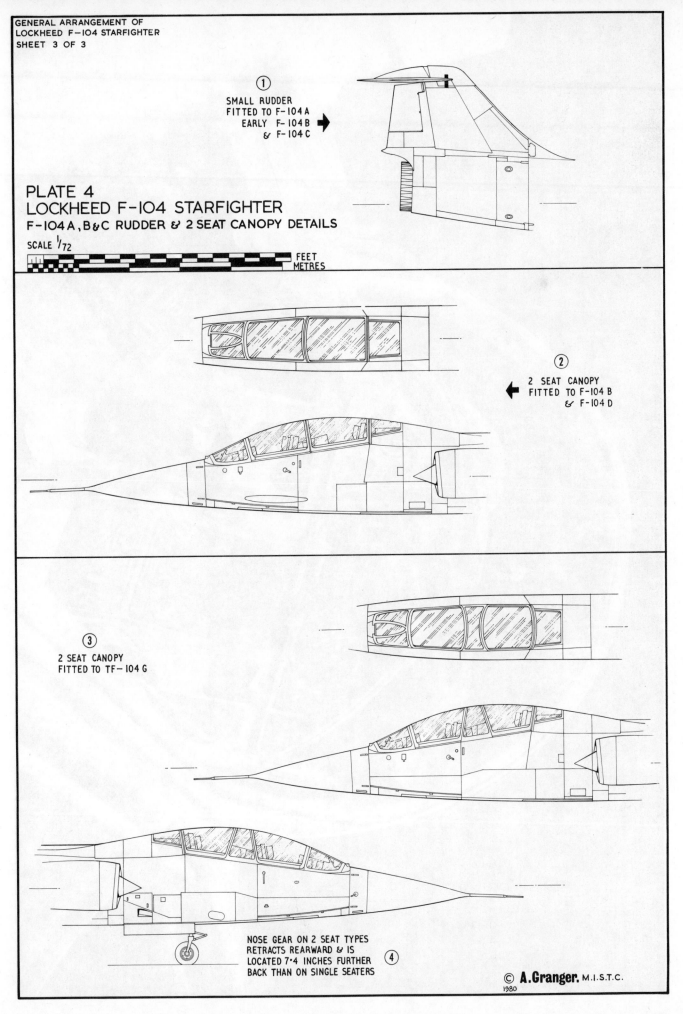

① SMALL RUDDER
FITTED TO F-IO4A
EARLY F-IO4B
& F-IO4C

PLATE 4
LOCKHEED F-IO4 STARFIGHTER
F-IO4A, B&C RUDDER & 2 SEAT CANOPY DETAILS

SCALE ¹/₇₂

FEET
METRES

② 2 SEAT CANOPY
FITTED TO F-IO4B
& F-IO4D

③ 2 SEAT CANOPY
FITTED TO TF—IO4 G

NOSE GEAR ON 2 SEAT TYPES
RETRACTS REARWARD & IS
LOCATED 7·4 INCHES FURTHER
BACK THAN ON SINGLE SEATERS ④

© A. Granger. M.I.S.T.C.
1980

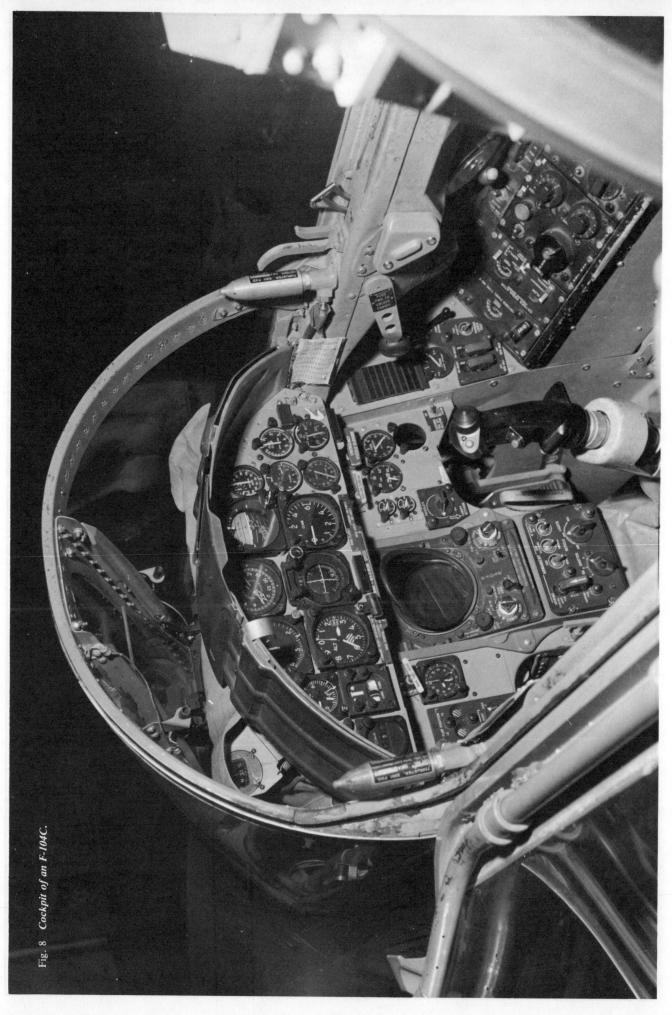

Fig. 8 *Cockpit of an F-104C.*

54

Fig. 9 Trio of F-104As armed with Sidewinder AAMs.

Fig. 10 A camouflaged F-104C on war service in Vietnam. Note flight refuelling probe.

Fig. 11 *Neat echelon formation of C models of the 479th Tactical Fighter Wing carrying centreline and wing-tip drop tanks.*

Fig. 12 *In this American Civil War centennial picture a tripod-mounted hand-cranked Gatling gun of 1861 is compared with the F-104's Gatling-type Vulcan cannon.*

Fig. 13 *Another echelon formation of F-104Cs of the 479th TFW. Note flight refuelling probe on the nose of the second machine.*

The single-seat F-104C (77 built) and also the two-seat D (21 built) were developed for Tactical Air Command, and featured 15,000lb (6804kg) thrust afterburning J79-GE-7 engines, blown flaps to increase lift and shorten the landing run, provision for in-flight probe-and-drogue refuelling, and equipment for ground-attack work. The C had a 25 per cent increase in vertical tail area and the rudder was powered and provided both yaw-damping and directional control with a single surface. Both these modifications were first introduced on late-production F-104Bs.

The F-104C served with but one Tactical Air Command wing, the 479th at George AFB, California, which deployed some of its aircraft to Vietnam in 1964 to counter the threat posed by MiG fighters. In the event, the F-104Cs were employed mostly on ground attack and the type was withdrawn at the end of 1965, only to be returned to Vietnam in 1966 following the début of the MiG-21 in North Vietnamese service.

Japan bought 20 F-104DJ trainers for assembly by Mitsubishi for the Japanese Air Self-Defence Force. Another two-seater based on the D model was the F-104F, 30 of which were delivered by Lockheed to the Federal German Luftwaffe.

As early as 7 May 1958, a YF-104A flying from Palmdale set a world altitude record of 91,249ft (28470m), and on 14 December 1959 an F-104C took the record to 103,389ft (31513m). The Starfighter's high-altitude capabilities were further enhanced in 1963 when three F-104As were converted to NF-104As with rocket boost, one setting a world record of nearly 119,000ft (36273m) in that year. The NF-104As were used at the

Fig. 14 *Three F-104As were converted to NF-104As with rocket boost in 1963 and one of them set a world altitude record of nearly 119,000ft (36273m) that same year.*

Fig. 15 *An F-104F in Luftwaffe insignia. Although the Starfighter is notorious for its high accident rate in Luftwaffe service, the type is technically sound and is certainly one of the most remarkable aircraft yet built.* Fig. 16 *An RF-104G of 306 Squadron, Royal Netherlands Air Force, displays the camera fairing below the forward fuselage as it banks over the Dutch countryside.*

USAF Aerospace Research Pilots School at Edwards AFB, California. Three other Starfighters were used by the National Aerospace and Space Administration for astronaut training with the designation F-104N.

Ex-USAF Starfighters were supplied to Taiwan and Pakistan, some of the latter's machines seeing action in the air support role during the Indian-Pakistan conflict of September 1965.

Although little used in America, because the USAF considered it to be not as successful as the larger fighters which gradually appeared, the Starfighter generated what was hitherto the greatest international co-operative venture in the history of the aerospace business. The seeds of this were sown in 1958 when Lockheed developed, as a company-financed project, the Mach 2.2 F-104G, aimed primarily at a German requirement for a close-support strike fighter.

Based on the F-104C, this featured an uprated engine, a much strengthened structure, increased vertical tail area as on the F-104B and D, manoeuvring flaps, very complete radar and electronics (for gunnery, rocket-firing, bombing and navigation), and manoeuvring auto-pilot, an upwards (instead of downwards) ejection seat, and provision for bigger and more versatile warloads.

In March 1959 Germany signed a contract with Lockheed for development of the F-104G and its subsequent production under licence in Germany, but eventually the plans were modified and the F-104G was built by German, Dutch and Belgian consortia for the Luftwaffe and Marineflieger (604), the Royal Netherlands Air Force (95) and the Belgian Air Force (99); and for the Italian Air Force (124) by an Italian consortium led by Fiat. In addition, Germany obtained a further 96 F-104Gs from Lockheed, while Belgium and Italy obtained one each, these machines being supplied through the Military Assistance Programme. Lockheed flew the first F-104G at Burbank on 5 October 1960 and delivery to Germany began in May 1961. The first European-built F-104G followed in August, from the German consortium.

As part of the US Military Assistance Programme, Canadair built 140 US-financed F-104Gs for supply to Denmark (25), Greece (36), Norway (16), Spain (25) and Turkey (38). The first of these flew at Montreal on 30 July 1963 and followed production of 200 basically G-model Starfighters, but minus the Vulcan cannon, for the RCAF, which for a short time called them CF-111s before redesignating them CF-104s. The RCAF also received 38 Lockheed-built CF-104D trainers, which again were based on the F-104G.

Basically similar to the F-104G but equipped primarily as an interceptor is the JASDF's F-104J, three of which were built by Lockheed (first flight 30 June 1961) and a further 207 built by Mitsubishi in Japan.

A two-seat version of the F-104G was developed by Lockheed as the TF-104G and 167 were supplied to Germany, 14 to the Netherlands and 29 to other European air forces. Yet another variant of the G model is the RF-104G multi-role reconnaissance aircraft.

The sole type of Starfighter built new since 1967 has

Fig. 17 *A CF-104 from RCAF Station Cold Lake carrying a reconnaissance pod containing four 70mm Vinten cameras.* Fig. 18 *A QF-104A target drone – in this case piloted.*

been the Italian F-104S, basically an air-superiority fighter armed with two Raytheon Sparrow air-to-air missiles (hence the suffix letter "S") but also used as a fighter-bomber. Developed jointly by Lockheed and Fiat/Aeritalia, this model has a more powerful J79 engine, nine external stores points, and can attain Mach 2.4. The first of two Lockheed-built prototypes flew in 1966, and between 1969 and 1979, when production ceased, 246 F-104Ss were manufactured in Italy. The Italian Air Force took 206 and the rest went to Turkey.

The world-wide total of Starfighters built was 2,583, including the two XF-104s

At given periods over more than two decades the Starfighter has been the principal fighter aircraft flown by 15 different nations: Belgium, Canada, Denmark, West Germany, Greece, Italy, Japan, Jordan, the Netherlands, Norway, Pakistan, Spain, Taiwan, Turkey and the USA. It remained in the USAF's inventory until January 1974, but many countries will retain the Starfighter in their operational inventories until the mid-1980s.

SPECIFICATION – F-104G

Powerplant: One 15,800lb (7165kg) thrust General Electric J79-11A turbojet with reheat.
Dimensions: Span (less tip tanks) 21ft 11in (6680mm); length 54ft 9in (16688mm); height 13ft 6in (4115mm).
Weights: Empty, 14,082lb (6387kg); maximum loaded, 28,779lb (13054kg).
Performance: Maximum speed 1,450mph (2,330km/h or Mach 2.2); initial climb 50,000ft (15250m)/min; service ceiling 58,000ft (17680m) (zoom ceiling over 90,000ft (27400m); range with maximum weapons approximately 300 miles (483km); range with four drop tanks (high altitude, subsonic) 1,380 miles (2220km).
Armament: Most versions have centreline rack capable of carrying 2,000lb (907kg) and two underwing pylons each rated at 1,000lb (454kg); additional racks for small missiles such as Sidewinder on fuselage, under wings or on tips. Certain versions have reduced fuel and one 20mm M-61 Vulcan rotary cannon in fuselage.

Fig. 19 *The prototype of Italy's F-104S Super Starfighter on the ramp at Palmdale in 1967 carrying advanced Sparrow radar-guided missiles.*

GENERAL DYNAMICS
F-16 FIGHTING FALCON

By Philip J. R. Moyes

Fig. 1 *An F-16A (left) and a two-seat F-16B fighter/trainer.* [All photographs courtesy General Dynamics.]

Fig. 2 *A pair of F-16As in a near-vertical climb. The F-16 pilot can use the aircraft's instantaneous and sustained 9g manoeuvre capability to force the enemy into high-g energy dissipating manoeuvres while he maintains a commanding advantage in turn rate and acceleration rates.*

Fig. 3 *In this view of the second YF-16 on test, the marque's superbly blended wing-fuselage is seen to advantage. Note the aperture for the 20mm cannon in the port strake.*

One of the most important combat aircraft of the 1980s and beyond, the F-16 Fighting Falcon represents a highly successful attempt by General Dynamics to produce a new-generation, single-engined, single-seat, multi-role lightweight tactical fighter to complement the relatively heavy, elaborately equipped and expensive McDonnell Douglas F-15 Eagle (*Aerodata International No 13*).

The Fighting Falcon's manoeuvrability and combat radius exceed that of all threat aircraft while operating in the air superiority role: In an air-to-surface role, it has an exceptional mission radius of over 500 nautical miles (926km), superior weapons delivery accuracy, and an excellent self-defence capability. Because the F-16 is small, it is difficult to detect, visually or with radar, and hard to hit.

Contributing to its superiority in the air combat role and providing the basic qualities required for the air-to-ground role are the low wing loading, high-thrust engine – the Pratt & Whitney F100 which was developed and proved on the F-15 – and rugged structure. Added to these essential qualities are an advanced digital fire con-

trol and stores management system and nine store stations with capacity for the carriage of up to 15,200lb (6895kg) of external stores. The result is a superior multimission air-to-air and air-to-ground tactical fighter. The F-16 has been dubbed the Swing Force Fighter because of its ability to easily swing from one role to another.

Spanning 32ft 10in (10008mm) overall with tip-mounted AIM-9 Sidewinder missiles, 49ft 5.9in (15085mm) long and having a basic design gross weight of 22,500lb (10206kg), the altogether exciting Fighting Falcon was originally begun as a technology demonstrator, two prototypes being ordered in April 1972 under the United States Air Force's Lightweight Fighter (LWF) programme. The first YF-16 flew on 20 January 1974 followed by the second on 9 May, by which time the LWF programme had become the Air Combat Fighter (ACF) programme with the promise of an initial USAF order for 650 of the winning design, with an extensive support depot in Europe.

The F-16 was eventually declared the winner of the ACF competition in January 1975, the main factors

Fig. 4 *The second YF-16 formating with two Convair F-106A Delta Darts.*

behind its selection being its overwhelming performance and life cycle cost advantages over its competitor, the Northrop YF-17. Six months later, the F-16 was chosen by four European members of NATO – Belgium, Denmark, Holland and Norway – to replace their ageing Lockheed F-104s (*Aerodata International* No 15). Also during that year came the start of a vast co-production programme – the largest international military co-production programme in history – wherein the industries of the United States and the four European nations just mentioned would share in the manufacture of the F-16.

Today, assembly lines are in operation at Fort Worth, Texas; Gosselies, Belgium; and near Amsterdam, Holland. There are 33 major subcontractors in the four European industrial partner nations, and these firms, in turn, have placed second tier F-16 subcontracts with nearly 400 additional European firms. General Dynamics, prime contractor for the Fighting Falcon, has placed subcontracts for F-16 work with some 4,000 US firms.

Some idea of the fine production rate is given by the fact that by August 1980 over 200 F-16s had rolled off the three production lines. At Fort Worth an unsurpassed quality mark was achieved when a truly "perfect" Fighting Falcon was delivered to the USAF – a machine which was found to be absolutely free of even minor defects after rigorous acceptance testing on the

ground and in flight. This rare milestone is considered virtually impossible to achieve because of the complex nature of the aircraft, and as far as is known it was the first time in the Fort Worth Division's entire history that it had delivered a plane with absolutely no discrepancies.

In August 1978 Israel announced her intention of acquiring F-16s as the newest addition to her fighter force. Seventy-five aircraft were specified for the first buy with potential for more later on. The F-16 has been in operational status with the USAF and the Air Forces of Holland and Belgium since 1979, and with the Danish, Norwegian and Israeli air forces since 1980.

The F-16 is due to enter service with the Egyptian Air Force in early 1982, and at the time of writing (March 1981) has also been ordered by the South Korean Air Force. Three countries currently considering possible purchase of F-16s are Austria, Australia and Spain. Total currently planned F-16 production runs to more than 1,850 aircraft of which 1,388 are for the USAF.

The Fighting Falcon incorporates a number of technologies and design innovations which have not previously been combined in a single aircraft. These include forebody strakes to generate vortices that permit buffet-free, divergent-free flight at high angles of attack; wing-body blending for both increased lift and internal volume for fuel and essential mechanical and avionic equipment; fly-by-wire – a complete electronic

Fig. 5 *This F-16A may well be the first defect-free (roll-out to delivery) military aircraft ever produced. Tail codes "HL" signify Hill AFB, Utah.* Fig. 6 *F-16s on the production line at Fort Worth.*

flight control system; relaxed static stability – control-configured vehicle; variable wing camber – automatic leading-edge manoeuvring flaps; side-stick controller – easy and accurate control at high 'g'; high acceleration/high visibility cockpit – tailored to meet the pilot's needs.

The technologies applied to the F-16 were selected and integrated in such a fashion as to simplify the aircraft and reduce weight by several thousand pounds, thus reducing the basic cost. In addition, the light weight of the aircraft is achieved without extensive use of exotic materials or degradation in strength.

The modular design approach – the forward fuselage, the inlet, the centre fuselage, the aft fuselage, the tail unit, and the wings are designed as modules – provides for ease of manufacture, growth and upgrading of technology. The airframe is basically of conventional, riveted sheet metal construction and is over 80% aluminium with selective use of graphite composites. Fuselage construction is of sheet metal skins stiffened by formed and built-up sheet metal frames and longerons. In areas where concentrated loads or functional requirements dictate, integrally machined bulkheads, spars, or beams are used. Each wing skin is a single machined plate. Bonded construction is limited to the wing control surfaces, rudder, leading edge of the vertical fin, horizontal tail, and secondary structure.

Design load limit of the F-16 is 9g with 100% internal fuel, in contrast to current fighters with design load limits of 6.5g to 7.3g with 60 to 80% internal fuel.

Fig. 7 *The F-16 pictured with an array of bombs, fuel tanks and other stores.*

Standard armament of the Fighting Falcon is a 20mm rapid-fire (6,000 rounds per minute) Vulcan M61 cannon, housed in the port leading edge strake, and AIM-9 Sidewinder infra-red heat-seeking air-to-air missiles (AAMs). Six AIM-9s can be carried on external store stations and need not be down-loaded for air-to-surface missions. Sparrow and Sky Flash all-weather AAMs have also been launched from a F-16 prototype. The Fighting Falcon is also capable of deploying a wide range of other external ordnance, from USAF inventory missile launchers and bomb racks carried on its nine ordnance stations − one of which is located on the fuselage centreline, six being under the wings and two on the wing tips. The pylons can accommodate a maximum payload capacity of 15,200lb (6,895kg) of fuel tanks, conventional free-fall bombs and dispenser weapons, the latest in laser and TV-guided munitions, countermeasure pods, and other special payloads.

The F-16's avionics complement is designed to provide effective performance for both air-to-air and air-to-surface missions. The fire control system − including radar, head-up display, and pilot controls − has been configured for "eyes out of the cockpit" operation to eliminate any requirements for the pilot to look away from the target. The key fire controls have been integrated to provide the pilot with quick-reaction, fingertip control of displays and weapons from the throttle, flight control stick, and integrated stores management set.

Fig. 8 *Nine store stations provide versatility and large capacity.*

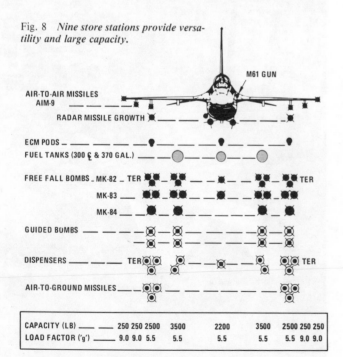

HARD POINT CAPACITY = 15,200 LBS

Fig. 9 *F-16 maintenance requirements have been minimised by the use of extensive built-in tests, self-tests, and status indicators, and by the provision of quick-access panels for inspection and servicing. Sixty per cent of the aircraft's surface is removable.*

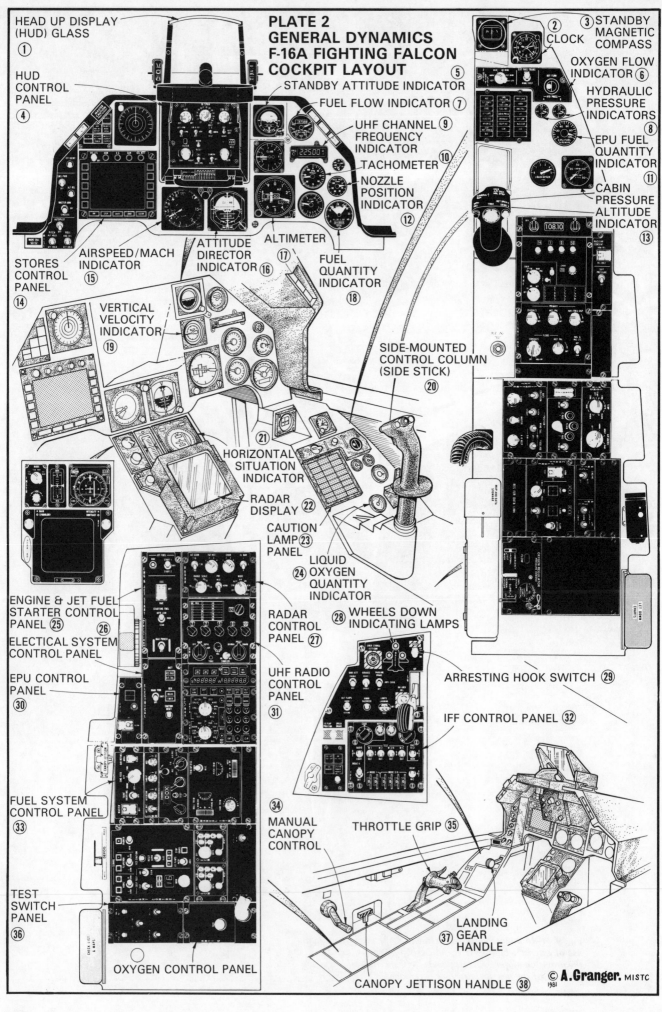

**PLATE 2
GENERAL DYNAMICS
F-16A FIGHTING FALCON
COCKPIT LAYOUT**

1. HEAD UP DISPLAY (HUD) GLASS
2. CLOCK
3. STANDBY MAGNETIC COMPASS
4. HUD CONTROL PANEL
5. STANDBY ATTITUDE INDICATOR
6. OXYGEN FLOW INDICATOR
7. FUEL FLOW INDICATOR
8. HYDRAULIC PRESSURE INDICATORS
9. UHF CHANNEL FREQUENCY INDICATOR
10. TACHOMETER
11. EPU FUEL QUANTITY INDICATOR
12. NOZZLE POSITION INDICATOR
13. CABIN PRESSURE ALTITUDE INDICATOR
14. STORES CONTROL PANEL
15. AIRSPEED/MACH INDICATOR
16. ATTITUDE DIRECTOR INDICATOR
17. ALTIMETER
18. FUEL QUANTITY INDICATOR
19. VERTICAL VELOCITY INDICATOR
20. SIDE-MOUNTED CONTROL COLUMN (SIDE STICK)
21. HORIZONTAL SITUATION INDICATOR
22. RADAR DISPLAY
23. CAUTION LAMP PANEL
24. LIQUID OXYGEN QUANTITY INDICATOR
25. ENGINE & JET FUEL STARTER CONTROL PANEL
26. ELECTICAL SYSTEM CONTROL PANEL
27. RADAR CONTROL PANEL
28. WHEELS DOWN INDICATING LAMPS
29. ARRESTING HOOK SWITCH
30. EPU CONTROL PANEL
31. UHF RADIO CONTROL PANEL
32. IFF CONTROL PANEL
33. FUEL SYSTEM CONTROL PANEL
34. MANUAL CANOPY CONTROL
35. THROTTLE GRIP
36. TEST SWITCH PANEL
37. LANDING GEAR HANDLE
38. CANOPY JETTISON HANDLE

OXYGEN CONTROL PANEL

© A. Granger. MISTC 1981

PLATE 1

GENERAL DYNAMICS F-16A FIGHTING FALCON
LA TSVAH HAGANA LE ISRAEL/HEYL HA'AVIR
(ISRAELI DEFENCE FORCE/AIR FORCE)

SCALE 1/96

RESEARCH: A. GRANGER ©
ARTWORK: ROY MILLS 1981

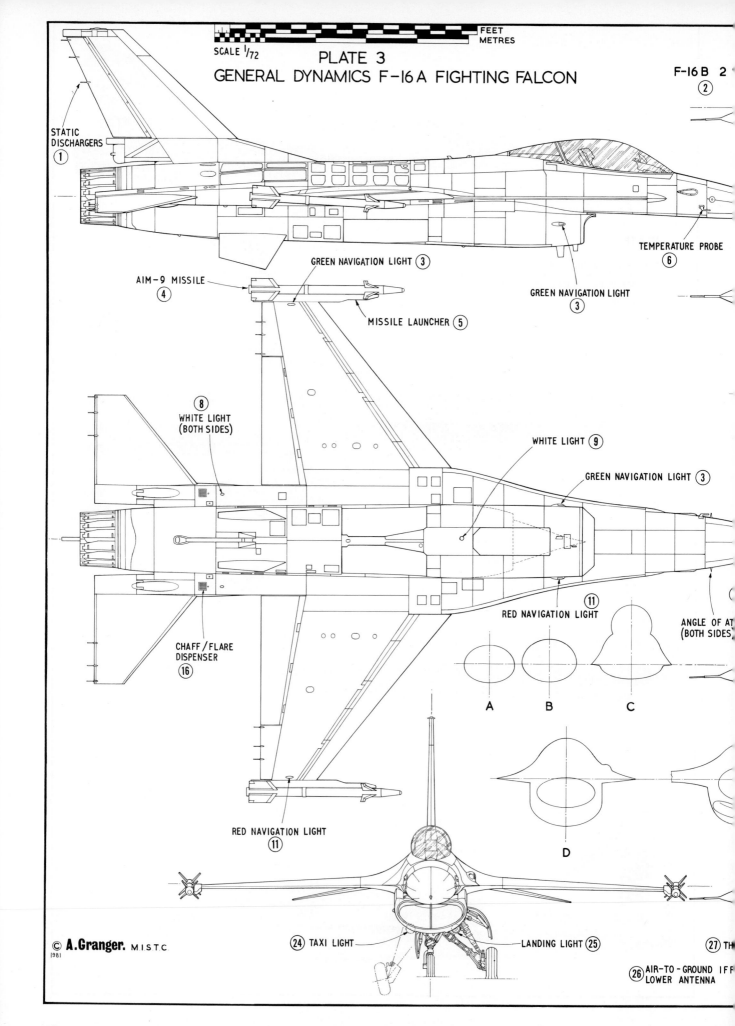

SCALE 1/72

FEET
METRES

PLATE 3
GENERAL DYNAMICS F-16A FIGHTING FALCON

F-16B 2
②

STATIC
DISCHARGERS
①

TEMPERATURE PROBE
⑥

AIM-9 MISSILE
④

GREEN NAVIGATION LIGHT ③

GREEN NAVIGATION LIGHT
③

MISSILE LAUNCHER ⑤

⑧
WHITE LIGHT
(BOTH SIDES)

WHITE LIGHT ⑨

GREEN NAVIGATION LIGHT ③

RED NAVIGATION LIGHT
⑪

ANGLE OF AT
(BOTH SIDES)

CHAFF/FLARE
DISPENSER
⑯

A   B   C

D

RED NAVIGATION LIGHT
⑪

© A.Granger. MISTC
1981

㉔ TAXI LIGHT

LANDING LIGHT ㉕

㉗ TH

㉖ AIR-TO-GROUND IFF
LOWER ANTENNA

70

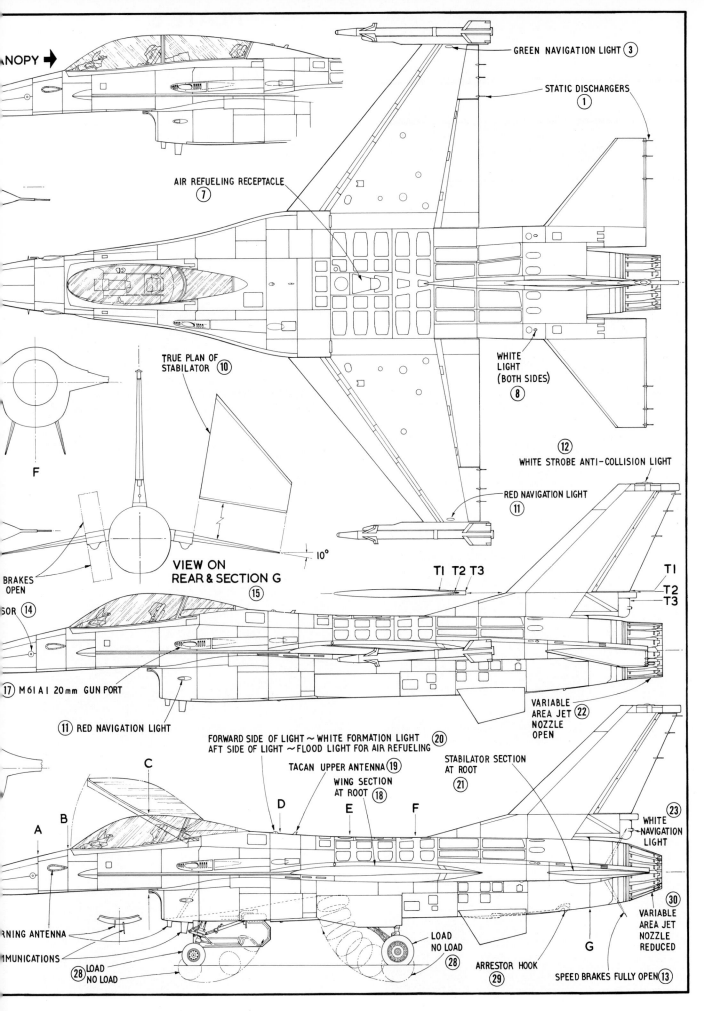

CANOPY →

GREEN NAVIGATION LIGHT ③

STATIC DISCHARGERS ①

AIR REFUELING RECEPTACLE ⑦

TRUE PLAN OF STABILATOR ⑩

WHITE LIGHT (BOTH SIDES) ⑧

⑫ WHITE STROBE ANTI-COLLISION LIGHT

RED NAVIGATION LIGHT ⑪

F

BRAKES OPEN

SOR ⑭

10°

VIEW ON REAR & SECTION G ⑮

T1 T2 T3

T1 T2 T3

⑰ M 61 A1 20mm GUN PORT

VARIABLE AREA JET ② NOZZLE OPEN

⑪ RED NAVIGATION LIGHT

FORWARD SIDE OF LIGHT ~ WHITE FORMATION LIGHT ⑳ AFT SIDE OF LIGHT ~ FLOOD LIGHT FOR AIR REFUELING

TACAN UPPER ANTENNA ⑲

WING SECTION AT ROOT ⑱

STABILATOR SECTION AT ROOT ㉑

C

D

E

F

A

B

㉓ WHITE NAVIGATION LIGHT

NING ANTENNA

MUNICATIONS

㉚

VARIABLE AREA JET NOZZLE REDUCED

G

㉘ LOAD NO LOAD

LOAD NO LOAD ㉘

ARRESTOR HOOK ㉙

SPEED BRAKES FULLY OPEN ⑬

71

PLATE 5

A. *USAF F-16A of 388th Tactical Fighter Wing, Hill AFB.*

B & C. *First F-16B supplied to Israeli Defence Force/Air Force (La Tsvah Hagana Le Israel/Heyl Ha'Avir).*

D. *F-16A of Royal Norwegian Air Force (Kongelige Norske Luftforsvaret).*

E. *Belgian Air Force (Force Aérienne Belge) F-16A.*

F. *F-16B 2-seater of Royal Danish Air Force (Kongelige Danske Flyvevåben).*

G. *F-16A of Royal Netherlands Air Force (Koninklijke Luchtmacht).*

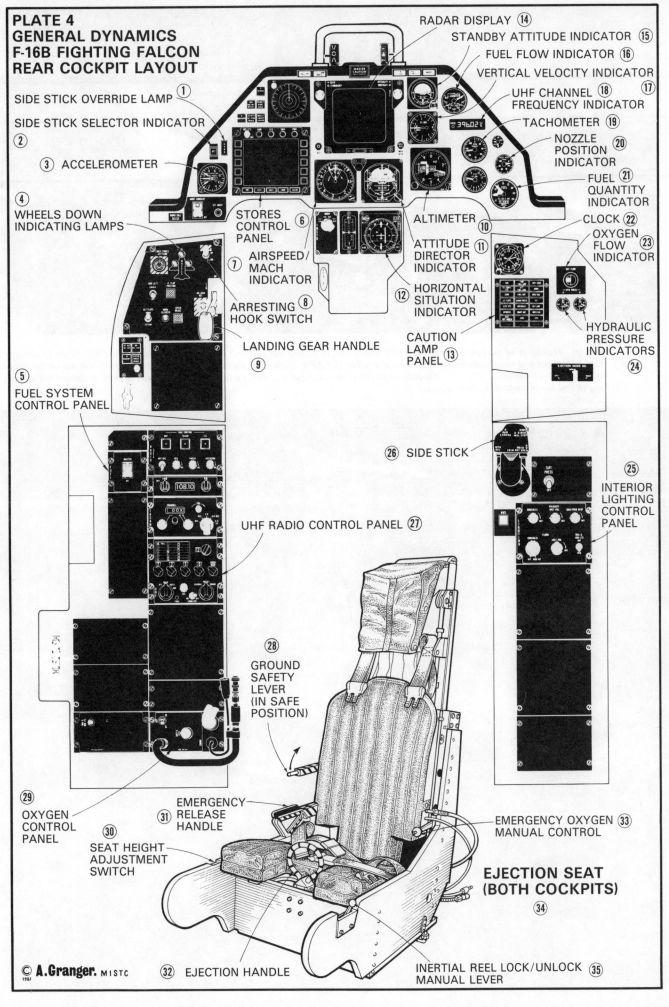

PLATE 4
GENERAL DYNAMICS
F-16B FIGHTING FALCON
REAR COCKPIT LAYOUT

RADAR DISPLAY ⑭
STANDBY ATTITUDE INDICATOR ⑮
FUEL FLOW INDICATOR ⑯
VERTICAL VELOCITY INDICATOR ⑰
UHF CHANNEL ⑱
FREQUENCY INDICATOR
TACHOMETER ⑲
NOZZLE ⑳
POSITION
INDICATOR
FUEL ㉑
QUANTITY
INDICATOR

SIDE STICK OVERRIDE LAMP ①

SIDE STICK SELECTOR INDICATOR
②

③ ACCELEROMETER

④

WHEELS DOWN
INDICATING LAMPS

STORES
CONTROL
PANEL ⑥

⑤
FUEL SYSTEM
CONTROL PANEL

AIRSPEED/
MACH
INDICATOR ⑦

ARRESTING
HOOK SWITCH ⑧

LANDING GEAR HANDLE
⑨

ALTIMETER ⑩
ATTITUDE ⑪
DIRECTOR
INDICATOR
HORIZONTAL ⑫
SITUATION
INDICATOR

CAUTION
LAMP
PANEL ⑬

CLOCK ㉒
OXYGEN ㉓
FLOW
INDICATOR

HYDRAULIC
PRESSURE
INDICATORS

㉔

㉖ SIDE STICK

㉕
INTERIOR
LIGHTING
CONTROL
PANEL

UHF RADIO CONTROL PANEL ㉗

㉘
GROUND
SAFETY
LEVER
(IN SAFE
POSITION)

㉙
OXYGEN
CONTROL
PANEL

㉚
SEAT HEIGHT
ADJUSTMENT
SWITCH

㉛
EMERGENCY
RELEASE
HANDLE

EMERGENCY OXYGEN ㉝
MANUAL CONTROL

EJECTION SEAT
(BOTH COCKPITS)

㉞

© A.Granger. MISTC
1981

㉜ EJECTION HANDLE

INERTIAL REEL LOCK/UNLOCK ㉟
MANUAL LEVER

73

Fig. 10   *Handover of the Israeli Air Force's first four F-16s, including this two-seat B model, took place at Fort Worth on 31 January 1980. The first IAF pilots and maintenance personnel were trained at Hill AFB, Utah. This particular machine carried Israeli insignia on the upper and lower surfaces of both wings.*   Fig. 11   *The second Israeli F-16A, tail number 102, on test from Fort Worth in 1980. It carried USAF insignia on upper and lower surfaces of both wings.*

Fig. 12 *At one time, the second YF-16 sported an experimental white and pale blue camouflage scheme, as shown in this in-flight refuelling scene.*

The F-16's coherent, pulse doppler fire control radar, furnished by Westinghouse Electric Corporation, provides all-weather acquisition, detection and track of airborne targets under clear or ground clutter environments. For the air-to-surface mission, the radar provides real-beam and expanded ground map modes for all-weather target acquisition as well as doppler beam sharpening for 8:1 improvement in azimuth resolution. Multiple weapon delivery modes provide delivery accuracies superior to other fighters under visual conditions and second only to the General Dynamics F-111 under blind-bombing conditions.

The F-16 has a complete set of navigation equipment, including a highly accurate inertial navigation set. Communications include both UHF and VHF voice communications sets. The aircraft also has a passive threat-warning system with modular contermeasure pods to counter airborne or surface threats electronically.

The avionics and other subsystems incorporate advanced built-in self-test, fault isolation and condition indicators to reduce time and manpower needed for isolation and replacement of system components on the flight line. These and other efficient maintenance features allow the F-16 to be supported with fewer direct maintenance personnel than contemporary fighter aircraft.

The F-16 has sufficient range to get to the battle with enough combat fuel allowance to stay with the fight. Compared with the present-day fighter aircraft it will replace, the F-16 has over twice the combat radius on an air superiority mission with each aircraft carrying its design air-to-air armament and flying the same combat manoeuvres. One of its most attractive features is its unparalleled fuel economy. It consumes one-half of the fuel of an F-4 Phantom and 17% less than an F-104 Starfighter when performing the same mission. During an exercise in 1980, a clean F-16 from Hill AFB, Utah, flew 125 to 150 miles (201 to 241km) into exercise airspace, stayed on station 25 to 35 minutes, entered several engagements requiring the use of afterburner, returned to base and landed with 1,000lb (454kg) of the 6,900lb (3130kg) fuel load remaining!

Fig. 13 *Fine profile study of the Israeli Air Force's first F-16B.*

Fig. 14 An F-16B with a long-range fuel tank slung below its centreline releases a salvo of bombs.

Fig. 15 F-16Bs of the Dutch, Belgian, Norwegian and Danish Air Forces seen together at Hill AFB where European Participating Group (EPG) pilots are being trained.

77

Writing in *Air Force Magazine*, published by the US Air Force Association, Captain Wayne C Edwards, an F-16 instructor pilot with the 16th Tactical/Fighter Training Squadron at Hill AFB, says: "The F-16 undoubtedly belongs to a new generation. However, in terms of great fighters, most F-16 pilots believe that over the long run it will carve out its own place in the annals of fighter aviation. I envision it becoming like the P-51, F-86, or F-100 of previous generations – very prolific, well utilized because of its tremendous capabilities, and highly respected by the pilots lucky enough to fly it. There is, in my mind, simply no other airplane in the world today I would rather take into combat if it became necessary . . . This is the airplane I want to be teamed up with for the rest of my flying days."

Essentially similar to the single-seat F-16A multi-purpose fighter except for the aft cockpit is the two-seat F-16B fighter/trainer. The B model carries about 1,100 fewer pounds (499 fewer kg) of internal fuel but still surpasses earlier fighters in agility, range and endurance.

Scheduled to be available for delivery from 1983 is the F-16/79, a private venture intermediate export fighter powered by the 18,000lb (8165kg) thrust General Electric J79 engine and intended to replace the Northrop F-5E Tiger II in the air forces of those nations unable to afford – or barred from receiving – front-line aircraft like the F-16. The development aircraft, which first flew on 29 October 1980, is a modified pre-series F-16B, and has a revised fixed-ramp inlet and other major modifications to allow for the longer J79.

SPECIFICATION – F-16A

Powerplant: One 25,000lb-thrust Pratt & Whitney F-100 turbofan with reheat.
Dimensions: Span with missiles 32ft 10in (10008mm), 31ft (9449mm) without missiles; length 49ft 5.9in (15085mm); height 16ft 5.2in (5009mm).
Weights: Empty 15,140lb (6,870kg); maximum take-off 35,400lb (16,060kg).
Performance: Max speed at sea level, Mach 1.2; max speed at altitude, Mach 2-plus; service ceiling 60,000ft-plus (15,000m-plus).
Armament: See text and diagram.

Fig. 16   *In this 60deg climb-out study of an F-16B with afterburner lit on its P&W F100 turbofan, a vortex from the leading edge can be seen across the top of the inboard wing surface, underlining the lift-generating capabilities of the strakes at low speed and high angles of attack.*

Fig. 17 *A 30deg inclined seat and raised heel-rest line increase the F-16 pilot's visibility, winning high praise from pilots for comfort. The low canopy rails and the bubble canopy itself permit almost unlimited visibility.*

Fig. 18 *Specks on the canopy aren't tolerated. This American airman is cleaning off loose dust that might cause trouble. Prominent is the British Marconi-Elliott head-up display.*

Fig. 19 *A revealing close-up of the inlet and undercarriage.*

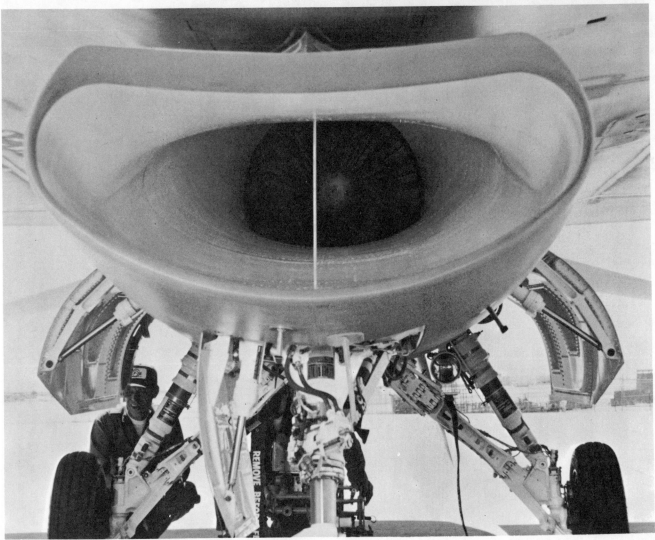

Fig. 20 One of four F-16s which visited Europe in 1979 to acquaint the European air forces with their new mount and to see if it would fit in their shelters.

GRUMMAN F-14A TOMCAT

By Philip J. R. Moyes

Fig. 1 *A pair of F-14As of the US Navy's VF-84 "Jolly Rogers" fighter squadron.* (All photos courtesy Grumman Aerospace Corpn unless otherwise credited.)

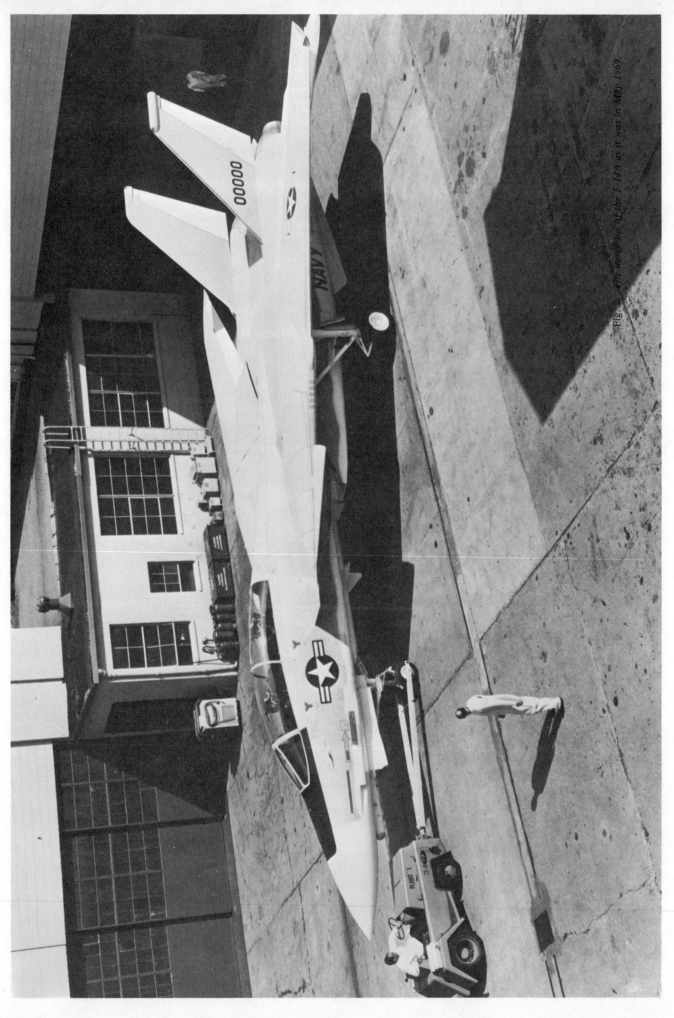

Fig. 7. The mock-up of the F-14A as it was in May 1969.

Fig. 3 *The second F-14A carrying its full armament load of six AIM-54 Phoenix missiles and two AIM-7 Sidewinders plus two external fuel tanks.*

The swing-wing, twin-engined F-14 Tomcat is the world's supreme interceptor fighter and is certain to remain so into the 1990s. Designed by Grumman Aerospace Corporation for the US Navy, it combines the speed and manoeuvrability of a dog-fighter with the unique detection and tracking capability of the Hughes AWG-9 weapons control system.

The AWG-9 track-while-scan radar gives the two-man crew of pilot and radar intercept officer the ability to track 24 enemy targets and simultaneously attack six different threats at varied altitudes and distances.

The F-14's versatility is evident in its varied armament capabilities. In addition to the internally-mounted M-61A Vulcan cannon capable of firing 4,000 or 6,000 rounds a minute, the Tomcat can be equipped with any combination of three air-to-air missiles: the long-range Phoenix, the medium-range AIM Sparrow and the short-range heat-seeking Sidewinder, as well as a variety of air-to-ground ordnance.

Guided by the AWG-9 system, the F-14-launched Phoenix missile has intercepted targets at distances of over 100 miles (161km) and altitudes ranging from 50 feet (15m) to over 80,000 feet (24,383m). The average success rate with the Phoenix in US Navy trials is approximately 84 per cent.

Powered by two Pratt & Whitney TF-30 turbofan engines, each providing more than 20,000lb (9,072kg) of thrust, the variable-sweep wing Tomcat is capable of speeds in excess of Mach 2. Inherently controllable at high angles of attack, this twin-tail aircraft remains in stabilised flight at very low air speeds. It has been flown routinely to angles of attack in excess of 50 degrees.

The automatically-positioned wings sweep to 68 degrees for high-speed manoeuvring, but when fully extended permit take-offs and landings in less than 2,000 feet (610m), at speeds below 138mph (222km/h). Positioned by computer, the wing angle is dependent on the speed of the aircraft. Such automatic positioning is invaluable in combat manoeuvring as it optimises aircraft performance for various altitudes and speeds.

Fig. 4 *An early F-14A test aircraft with wings in fully-swept position presenting an almost true delta planform. The wings have an in-flight sweep range of 20-68 degrees, with a 75-deg "oversweep" position available primarily to ease hangar stowage.*

Fig. 5 Another view of an early Tomcat with wings swept to their 68-deg limit for high-speed manoeuvrability.

Fig. 6 *The 14th and 15th Tomcats (Bu Nos 158613 and '614 respectively) from the Naval Air Test Centre, Patuxent River, Maryland, pictured during the first carrier compatibility trials, held aboard the USS* Forrestal *during late June 1972.* Fig. 7 *Profile of a brand new F-14A on test.*

The F-14 weapons system has proven itself time and again in mock warfare exercises, providing the US Navy carrier battle groups with air superiority needed to back up US national policies and objectives. In 1980 testimony before the US Congress, Vice-Admiral Wesley L. MacDonald, Deputy Chief of Naval Operations (Air Warfare), highlighted the vital role of the F-14, stating, "The F-14A and its integral Phoenix missiles combine to form a fighting system that is without equal in the world today. This nonpareil system is now, and will be for many years to come, the front-line maritime air superiority platform. This system is the keystone of our naval presence in any confrontation with the Soviet Union."

The Tomcat was designed to meet a US Navy requirement for a new carrier-borne fighter designated VFX to replace the cancelled F-111B on which Grumman was General Dynamics' associate contractor. The VFX requirements called for a crew of two in tandem seating; two P&W TF30-P-412 engines; the AWG-9 weapon system; the ability to carry six Phoenix, or six Sparrows, and four Sidewinders, plus an internal M-61A Vulcan cannon; high fighter limit load factors exceeding those of the McDonnell Douglas F4J Phantom with Sparrow and Phoenix missiles; and compatability with the USS *Hancock*-class CVAs.

A formal request for proposals for the VFX went out in June 1968 to five US aerospace manufacturers, and Grumman and McDonnell Douglas were selected for final competition, the Grumman swing-wing 303E design becoming the winner in mid-January 1969. An initial contract, covering 12 research, development, test and evaluation F-14As, was signed on 3 February 1969,

and construction soon began at Grumman's Calverton, New York, plant.

Powered by two P&W TF30-P-412A turbofans, the prototype F-14A made its first flight on 21 December 1970, piloted by Grumman's chief test pilot Bob Smyth, with F-14 project pilot Bill Miller in the rear seat. The plane crashed only nine days later while making its second flight, following complete failure of the hydraulic circuits to the power controls, but fortunately both crew members ejected successfully. Flight testing was eventually resumed, with the second prototype, in

Figs. 8 & 9 *An F-14 is launched from the USS* Forrestal *during carrier compatibility trials, 26 November 1973.*

Figs. 10 & 11 *Roll-out and take-off of the 100th Tomcat from Grumman's Calverton, New York, facility, 4 November 1974. At that time Grumman was delivering F-14As to the US Navy at the rate of five per month.*

May 1971, and gradually 10 more research and development aircraft joined the programme.

Two further accidents occurred in the course of development flying. On 30 June 1972 Bill Miller was killed in the tenth F-14A when he left his pull-up too late and struck the sea while practising for an air display, and on 20 June 1973 another Tomcat was destroyed by an unarmed Sparrow missile that it had itself launched; the crew ejected safely, and following this accident more powerful cartridges were used to eject missiles.

The F-14A underwent its first deck trials and catapult launches from the USS *Forrestal* in June 1972. On 8 October that year deliveries began to the NAS Miramar (California)-based VF-124, a non-deployable training unit for both the Pacific and Atlantic Fleets, and six days later two fleet fighter squadrons—VF-1 and -2— were activated at Miramar for F-14 training, these joining the nuclear-powered Pacific Fleet carrier USS *Enterprise* in September 1974 for an eight-month deployment in the Western Pacific and Indian Ocean.

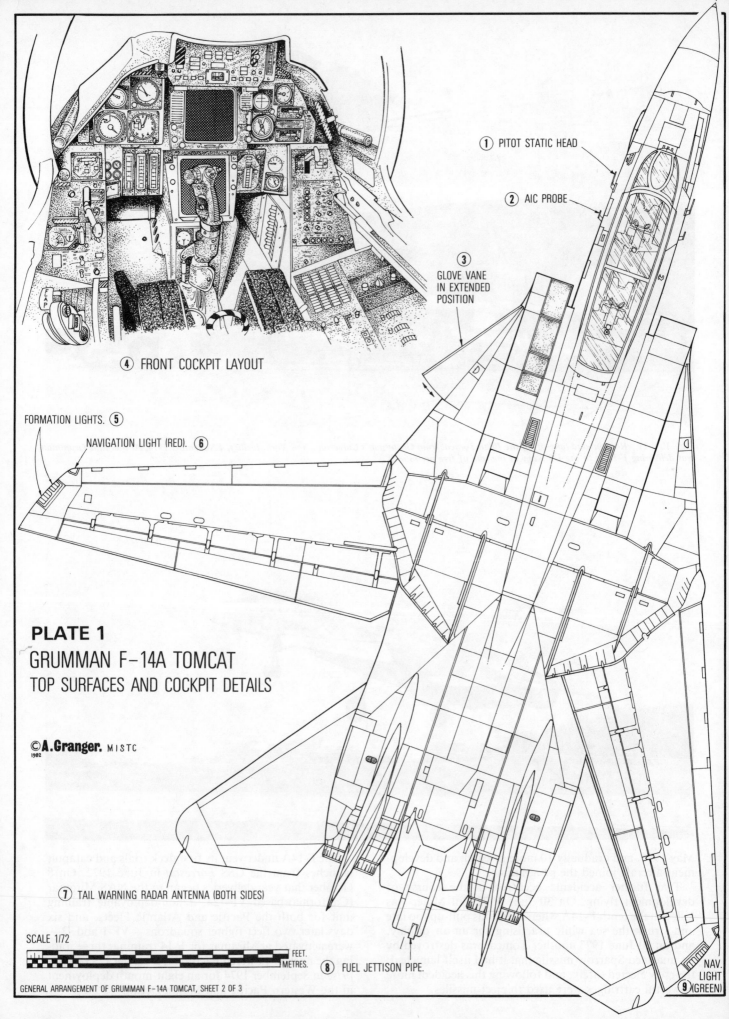

④ FRONT COCKPIT LAYOUT

① PITOT STATIC HEAD

② AIC PROBE

③ GLOVE VANE IN EXTENDED POSITION

FORMATION LIGHTS. ⑤

NAVIGATION LIGHT (RED). ⑥

PLATE 1
GRUMMAN F–14A TOMCAT
TOP SURFACES AND COCKPIT DETAILS

©**A.Granger.** MISTC
1982

⑦ TAIL WARNING RADAR ANTENNA (BOTH SIDES)

SCALE 1/72

FEET.
METRES.

⑧ FUEL JETTISON PIPE.

NAV. LIGHT ⑨ (GREEN)

GENERAL ARRANGEMENT OF GRUMMAN F-14A TOMCAT, SHEET 2 OF 3

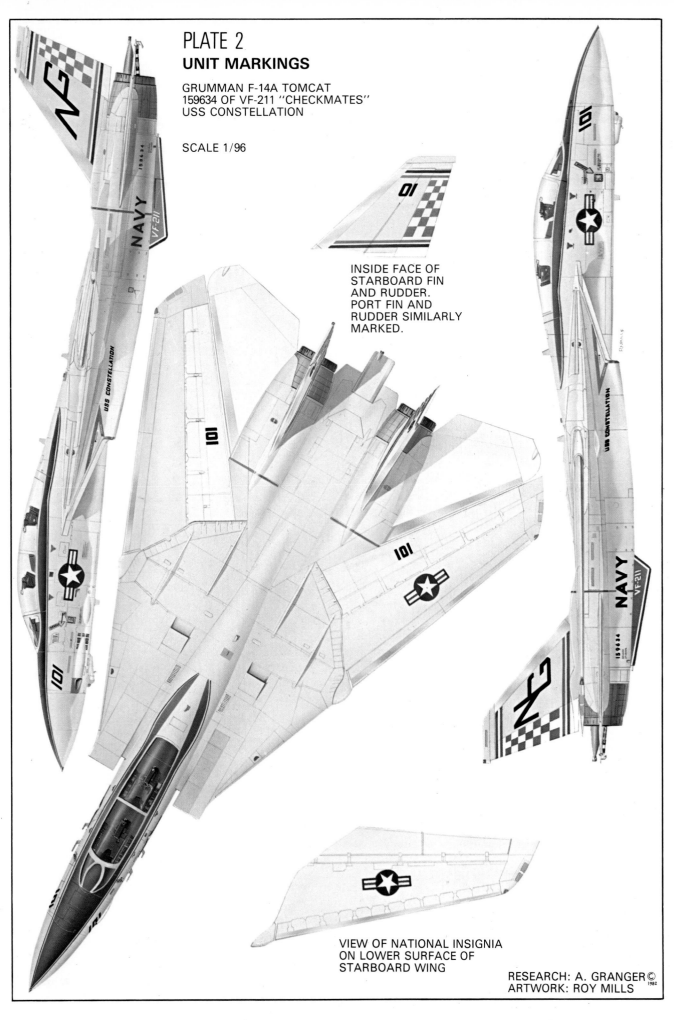

PLATE 2
UNIT MARKINGS

GRUMMAN F-14A TOMCAT
159634 OF VF-211 "CHECKMATES"
USS CONSTELLATION

SCALE 1/96

INSIDE FACE OF
STARBOARD FIN
AND RUDDER.
PORT FIN AND
RUDDER SIMILARLY
MARKED.

VIEW OF NATIONAL INSIGNIA
ON LOWER SURFACE OF
STARBOARD WING

RESEARCH: A. GRANGER ©
ARTWORK: ROY MILLS
1982

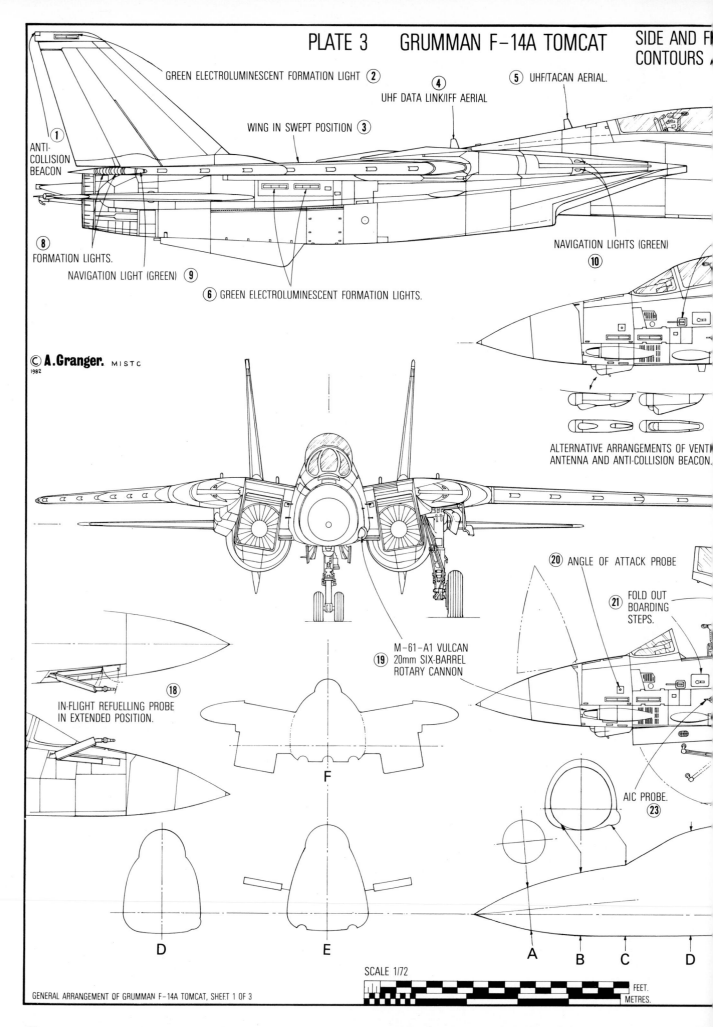

PLATE 3   GRUMMAN F-14A TOMCAT   SIDE AND F
CONTOURS

GREEN ELECTROLUMINESCENT FORMATION LIGHT ②

④ UHF DATA LINK/IFF AERIAL

⑤ UHF/TACAN AERIAL.

① WING IN SWEPT POSITION ③

ANTI-
COLLISION
BEACON

NAVIGATION LIGHTS (GREEN)

⑩

⑧

FORMATION LIGHTS.

NAVIGATION LIGHT (GREEN) ⑨

⑥ GREEN ELECTROLUMINESCENT FORMATION LIGHTS.

© A.Granger. MISTC
1982

ALTERNATIVE ARRANGEMENTS OF VENT
ANTENNA AND ANTI-COLLISION BEACON.

⑳ ANGLE OF ATTACK PROBE

㉑ FOLD OUT
BOARDING
STEPS.

M-61-A1 VULCAN
⑲ 20mm SIX-BARREL
ROTARY CANNON

⑱
IN-FLIGHT REFUELLING PROBE
IN EXTENDED POSITION.

AIC PROBE.
㉓

D

E

F

A   B   C   D

SCALE 1/72

FEET.

METRES.

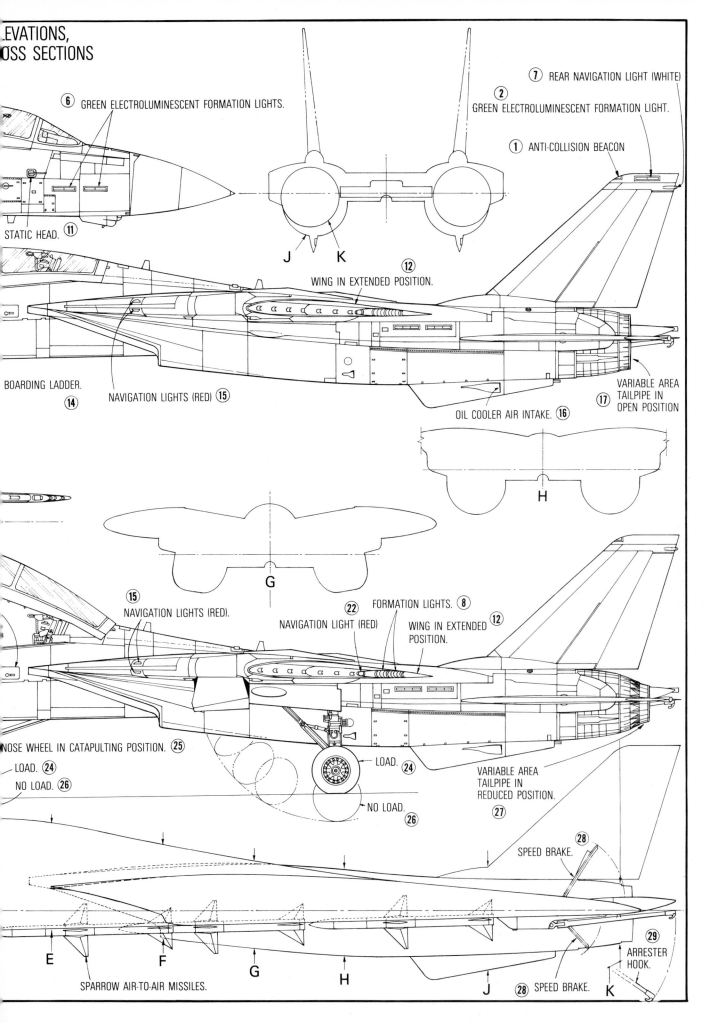

⑥ GREEN ELECTROLUMINESCENT FORMATION LIGHTS.

⑦ REAR NAVIGATION LIGHT (WHITE)

② GREEN ELECTROLUMINESCENT FORMATION LIGHT.

① ANTI-COLLISION BEACON

STATIC HEAD. ⑪

J   K

⑫ WING IN EXTENDED POSITION.

BOARDING LADDER. ⑭

NAVIGATION LIGHTS (RED) ⑮

OIL COOLER AIR INTAKE. ⑯

⑰ VARIABLE AREA TAILPIPE IN OPEN POSITION

H

G

⑮ NAVIGATION LIGHTS (RED).

②② NAVIGATION LIGHT (RED)

FORMATION LIGHTS. ⑧

WING IN EXTENDED POSITION. ⑫

NOSE WHEEL IN CATAPULTING POSITION. ②⑤

LOAD. ②④

LOAD. ②④

NO LOAD. ②⑥

NO LOAD. ②⑥

VARIABLE AREA TAILPIPE IN REDUCED POSITION. ②⑦

②⑧ SPEED BRAKE.

E   F   G   H   J   ②⑧ SPEED BRAKE.

②⑨ ARRESTER HOOK.

K

SPARROW AIR-TO-AIR MISSILES.

91

PLATE 4
UNIT MARKINGS

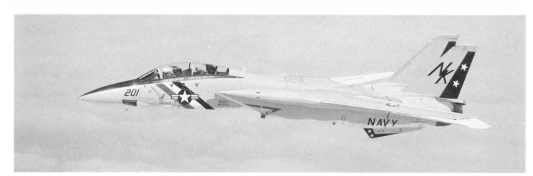

VF-2
USS *Enterprise*

VF-1
"Wolfpack"
USS *Enterprise*

VF-84
"Jolly Rogers"
USS *Nimitz*

VF-124
NAS *Miramar*

V-32
USS *John F. Kennedy*

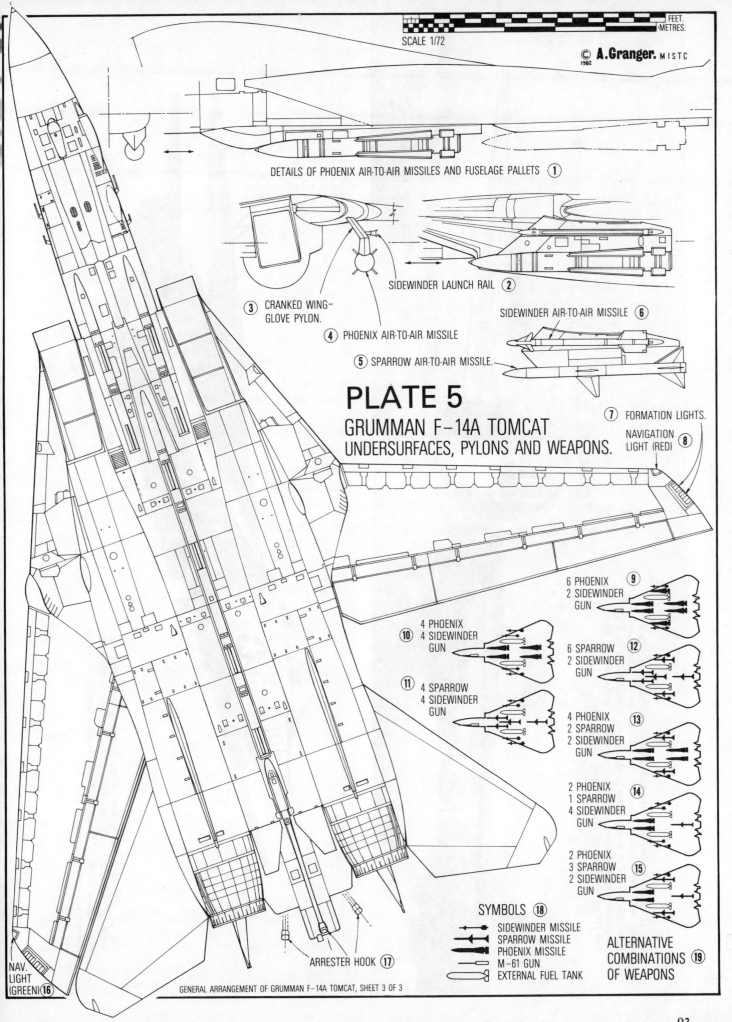

SCALE 1/72

© **A.Granger.** M I S T C
1982

DETAILS OF PHOENIX AIR-TO-AIR MISSILES AND FUSELAGE PALLETS ①

SIDEWINDER LAUNCH RAIL ②

③ CRANKED WING–GLOVE PYLON.

④ PHOENIX AIR-TO-AIR MISSILE

⑤ SPARROW AIR-TO-AIR MISSILE.

SIDEWINDER AIR-TO-AIR MISSILE ⑥

PLATE 5
GRUMMAN F–14A TOMCAT
UNDERSURFACES, PYLONS AND WEAPONS.

⑦ FORMATION LIGHTS.

⑧ NAVIGATION LIGHT (RED)

⑨ 6 PHOENIX 2 SIDEWINDER GUN

⑩ 4 PHOENIX 4 SIDEWINDER GUN

⑪ 4 SPARROW 4 SIDEWINDER GUN

⑫ 6 SPARROW 2 SIDEWINDER GUN

⑬ 4 PHOENIX 2 SPARROW 2 SIDEWINDER GUN

⑭ 2 PHOENIX 1 SPARROW 4 SIDEWINDER GUN

⑮ 2 PHOENIX 3 SPARROW 2 SIDEWINDER GUN

SYMBOLS ⑱

SIDEWINDER MISSILE
SPARROW MISSILE
PHOENIX MISSILE
M–61 GUN
EXTERNAL FUEL TANK

ALTERNATIVE COMBINATIONS OF WEAPONS ⑲

ARRESTER HOOK ⑰

NAV. LIGHT (GREEN) ⑯

GENERAL ARRANGEMENT OF GRUMMAN F–14A TOMCAT, SHEET 3 OF 3

Fig. 12 Large air intakes of the Tomcat are two-dimensional with a single mode of variable geometry through the use of computer-controlled scheduling ramps visible inside the tops of the intakes; these ramps travel up and down, depending on the speed of the aircraft, so that the air always enters at medium subsonic speeds.

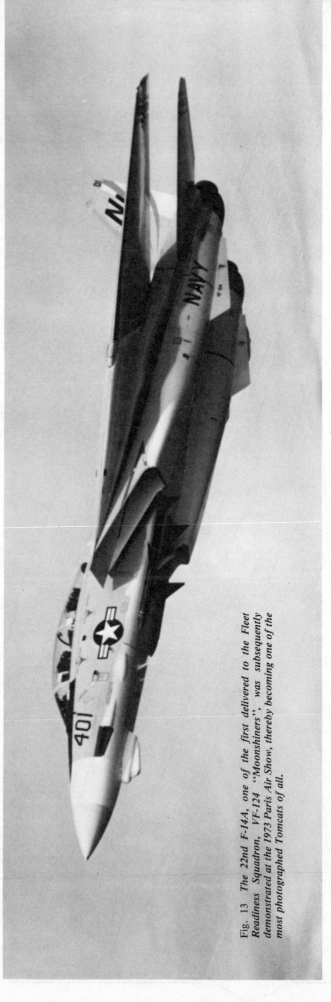

Fig. 13 The 22nd F-14A, one of the first delivered to the Fleet Readiness Squadron, VF-124 "Moonshiners", was subsequently demonstrated at the 1973 Paris Air Show, thereby becoming one of the most photographed Tomcats of all.

Fig. 14 *Close-up of an F-14A at NAS Miramar. Note preserved F6F Hellcat in background.* (US Navy)

Fig. 15 *Another view of the 22nd Tomcat in the markings of VF-124.*

Grumman ran into deep financial trouble during the early stages of the F-14 production programme due to the financial burden which arose from the original fixed-price plus incentive deal. In December 1972 the outlook was so grim that the company, having lost $135 million on the previous 86 Tomcats in Lots 1-4, refused to build the 48 in Lot 5 and demanded renegotiation of the contract. At first the US Navy refused, but eventually a compromise was reached, with a new price structure allowing for inflation, although Grumman had to accept a further loss of $105 million on Lot 5.

In early 1980, the F-14A was serving with 16 US Navy squadrons, spread between seven aircraft carriers and the Naval Air Stations at Miramar and Oceana, Virginia. At the time of writing, the US Navy plans to acquire a total of 521 Tomcats, equipping 18 squadrons, and in 1981 production was running at 30 aircraft per annum.

Following early fan blade failures on the TF30-P-412A, resulting in the loss of several F-14As, aircraft with the improved TF30-P-414 engine began to appear in mid-1977, starting with the 252nd machine. Previous aircraft have had their P-412As modified to the new standard.

Forty-nine US Navy F-14As are being fitted with the TARPS (Tactical Airborne Reconnaissance Pod System) so that three of the resulting F-14A/TARPS aircraft can be deployed with each carrier air wing, replacing the Rockwell RA-5C Vigilante and Vought RF-8G Crusader. The pod, which is mounted below the rear fuselage, houses a KS-87B frame camera for forward shots or verticals, a KA-99 panoramic camera and an AAD-5 infra-red scanner.

During 1976-78 eighty F-14As—differing from those in US Navy service only in the standard of their electronic countermeasures equipment — were supplied to

Fig. 16 *F-14A front cockpit.*

Fig. 17 *A Tomcat of VF-1 "Wolf Pack".*

Fig. 18 *F-14A rear cockpit.*   Fig. 19 *A Tomcat of VF-14 "Tophatters" pictured at some time between December 1975 and September 1976 when the unit was serving with the USS* John F Kennedy.

the Imperial Iranian Air Force to prevent overflights by Soviet Air Force MiG-25s. Following the overthrow of the Shah in 1979, US assistance was terminated and the Tomcat has seen little use in the protracted war with Iraq. Reports suggest that only a handful of the 75 F-14As held by the Iranian Islamic Revolutionary Air Force were still flying in mid-1981.

Fig. 20 *Trio of VF-84 Tomcats on a sortie when the unit was serving with the USS* Nimitz *in 1977.*

SPECIFICATION

Powerplant: Two Pratt & Whitney TF30-P-412A or P-414 turbofans each rated at 12,500lb st (5,670kgp) dry and 20,900lb st (9,480kgp) with afterburning.
Dimensions: Span (wings extended) 64ft 1½in (19.55m); span (maximum sweep) 37ft 7in (11.45m); span (oversweep on deck) 33ft 3½in (10.15m); length 61ft 11⅞in (18.90m); height 16ft 0in (4.88m).
Weights: Empty 39,930lb; loaded (intercept with four AIM-7F Sparrows) 58,904lb (26,718kg); (with six AIM-54A Phoenix) 69,790lb (31,656kg); combat air patrol 70,345lb (31,908kg); maximum 74,348lb (33,724kg).
Performance: Maximum speed (clean) 1,545mph (2,486km/h) or Mach 2.34; time to 60,000 ft (18,290m) 2 minutes 6 seconds; operating radius with four AIM-7F Sparrows 450 miles (725km).
Armament: See text and diagram.

Fig. 21 *An F-14A carrying four Phoenix, two Sparrow and two Sidewinder AAMs plus two external fuel tanks.*

Fig. 22 An F-14A carrying the TARPS (Tactical Airborne Reconnaissance Pod System). Note triangular glove vane which retracts into leading edge of fixed portion of wing and is automatically deployed above Mach 1.0, reaching its full extension of 15 degrees, at Mach 1.5. Unique to the Tomcat, these devices move the aerodynamic centre forward, reducing tailplane loads and improving manoeuvrability. For the latter purpose they can also be deployed by the pilot at lower speeds.

Fig. 23   *A VF-32 "Swordsmen" Tomcat armed with six Phoenix missiles.*

Fig. 24   *The first of the 80 F-14As to be delivered to Iran photographed on the occasion of its maiden flight from Calverton on 5 December 1975.*

NORTH AMERICAN F-100A
SUPER SABRE

By Philip J. R. Moyes

Fig. 1 *The fifth F-100A, incorporating redesigned fin and rudder (see narrative) shows off its 45-degree swept wings during a vertical climb.* (All photos courtesy of North American Aviation Corpn unless otherwise credited)

Fig. 2   *The first YF-100A, 52-5754, which first flew on 25 May 1953.*

To the North American F-100A went the distinction of being the world's first truly supersonic production aeroplane to see squadron service. Whereas the earlier F-86 Sabre and several of its swept-wing contemporaries could go supersonic in a dive, the F-100A could sustain speeds above Mach 1 in level flight.

First of the "Century Series" of fighters, the Super Sabre began as a company-funded design study based on the F-86D and was originally known as the Sabre 45, due to the wing sweepback being increased to 45 degrees. Work on the project commenced in February 1949, and the fighter was at first intended for the all-weather role. Following the début, in the Korean War, of the MiG-15, which was capable of outperforming the F-86, USAF demands for improved air superiority fighters increased. Accordingly, North American quicky adapted the Sabre 45 design to meet this need. The revised design was offered to the USAF in January 1951 and, after doing much additional work to satisfy Service requirements, North American was awarded an initial contract for two prototypes and 110 F-100A production aircraft on 1 November 1951.

The finalised Super Sabre, or "Hun" as the marque became popularly known in the USAF, resembled the F-86 only in general configuration and structural design. Powered by the new Pratt & Whitney J57 turbojet — which, with reheat, gave nearly three times the thrust available to the F-86 — the new fighter had a horizontal oval air intake in the nose of the low-drag fuselage and a single-piece clamshell cockpit canopy. All the internal fuel tanks were housed within the fuselage as was also the fixed armament of four 20 mm cannon. A large hydraulically-operated "barn-door" air-brake could be extended below the flat underside of the fuselage, level with the leading edge of the wing, and a drag-'chute, to reduce ground roll, could be deployed from a compartment under the tailplane. Most of the electronic equipment was housed in a large bay forward

Fig. 3 *Another view of the first YF-100A.*

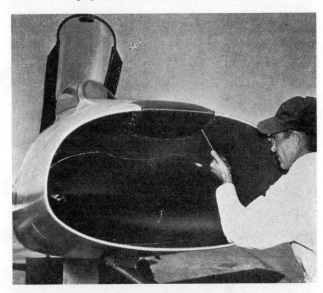

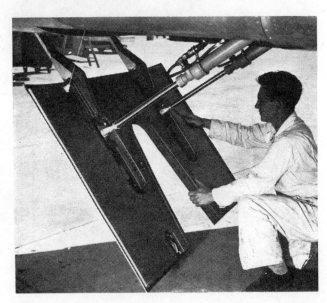

Fig. 4 *The Hun's air intake swallowed 250lb (68.94kg) of air per second and incorporated a gunsight aerial in the upper lip.*
Fig. 5 *"Barn door" speed brake was deployed by a pair of long-stroke hydraulic jacks acting in unison and apparently no change of trim resulted at any speed.*

Fig. 6 *Tail end of an F-100A with original stumpy fin and rudder. Slab tailplane is seen at full negative incidence.*

Fig. 7 *Lt Col F. K. "Pete" Everest, the Edwards AFB chief of flight test operations, pictured with the first YF-100A which he piloted to a world speed record of 755.149mph (1,215.287 km/h) over a 15km course at California's Salton Sea on 29 October 1953.*

Fig. 8 *George Welch, North American's chief test pilot, seen with the first YF-100A. He later lost his life in an early F-100A (52-5764) in one of the accidents which eventually were attributed to inertia coupling between the roll and yaw axes – a problem remedied by extending the vertical tail above the vortex caused by the canopy and slightly increasing the wing span.*

of the cockpit. The wing, of only six per cent thickness/chord ratio, featured automatic slots over most of the leading edge, and the trailing edge carried inboard ailerons; no flaps were fitted. Longitudinal control was achieved by movement of the horizontal slab tail located at the base of the fuselage and combining the functions of tailplane and elevators in one surface. The control system was hydraulically powered and irreversible.

The first of the two YF-100A prototypes was completed on 24 April 1953, and after being secretly transported from North American's Los Angeles plant to Edwards Air Force Base, California, it first took to the air on 25 May in the hands of the manufacturer's chief test pilot, George Welch. Mach 1 was exceeded on the first flight, and also on the second one made late that same day. The second YF-100A flew on 14 October 1953 and, like the first prototype, it had a P&W XJ-57-

Fig. 9 *An F-100A of the Air Development Centre, Wright Field, with the early stumpy vertical tail.* (Warren D Shipp)

Fig. 10 *This study of the first YF-100A shows to advantage the marque's flat underbelly.* Fig. 11 *A late production F-100A with tall vertical*
tail and standard underwing drop tanks.

Fig. 12 *Second production F-100A with leading edge slats extended.*

P7 engine and a taller fin and rudder than early production F-100As. The first of the latter was flown by George Welch on 29 October 1953, and on the same day the first YF-100A set a world speed record of 755.149 mph (1,215.287km/h) at Salton Sea, in California's Imperial Valley, piloted by Lt Col F K "Pete" Everest, the Edwards AFB chief of flight test operations. Because of the potential danger and difficulty in tracking a supersonic aircraft, and the improved performance of jet planes in thinner air, this was the last such record established at low altitude.

From September 1953, F-100As, with the 9,700lb (4,399.8kg) st J57-P-7 engine, were assigned to the 479th Day Fighter Wing of the USAF Tactical Air Command at George AFB, California, but the occurrence of several inexplicable accidents – one of which cost the life of George Welch – resulted in the Super Sabre being grounded three weeks later. After intensive investigation it was discovered that the accidents were due to inertia coupling between the roll and yaw axes, and the remedy involved the fitment of a new fin and rudder resembling that of the YF-100A, a slight increase in wing span – from 36ft 7in (11,151mm) to 38ft 9in (11,821mm) – and minor changes to the lateral and longitudinal control systems to improve pilot "feel".

These fixes were immediately initiated on the production line as well as being made to all the surviving examples of the 70 F-100As already delivered and were completely successful, the type being ungrounded in February 1955. Changes were made to the cockpit

Fig. 13 *An F-100A of the 1708th Ferrying Wing at Kelly AFB, Texas, with Wing insignia on tail and MATS insignia on rear fuselage.* (USAF)

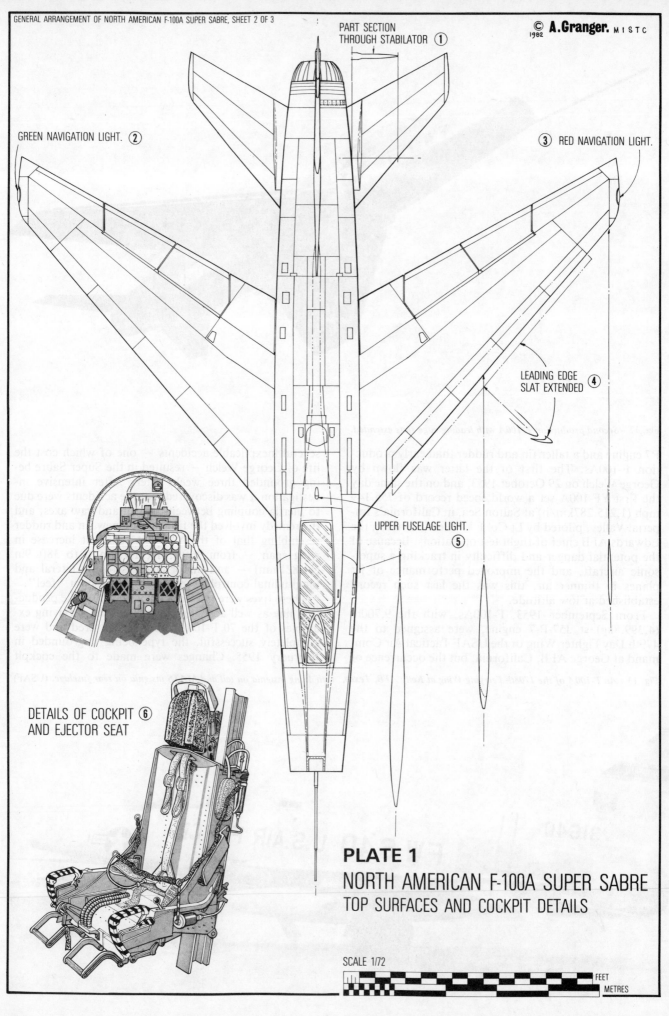

© A.Granger. M I S T C
1982

PART SECTION
THROUGH STABILATOR ①

GREEN NAVIGATION LIGHT. ②

③ RED NAVIGATION LIGHT.

LEADING EDGE
SLAT EXTENDED ④

UPPER FUSELAGE LIGHT.
⑤

DETAILS OF COCKPIT ⑥
AND EJECTOR SEAT

PLATE 1

NORTH AMERICAN F-100A SUPER SABRE
TOP SURFACES AND COCKPIT DETAILS

SCALE 1/72

FEET
METRES

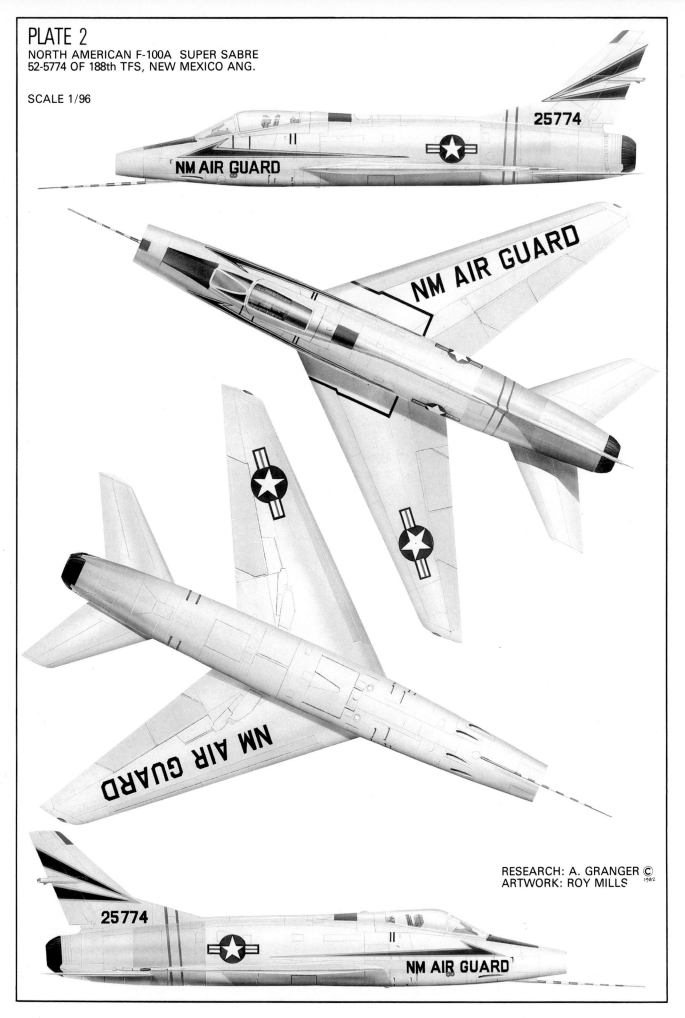

PLATE 2
NORTH AMERICAN F-100A SUPER SABRE
52-5774 OF 188th TFS, NEW MEXICO ANG.

SCALE 1/96

25774

NM AIR GUARD

NM AIR GUARD

NM AIR GUARD

25774

RESEARCH: A. GRANGER ©
ARTWORK: ROY MILLS
1982

25774

NM AIR GUARD

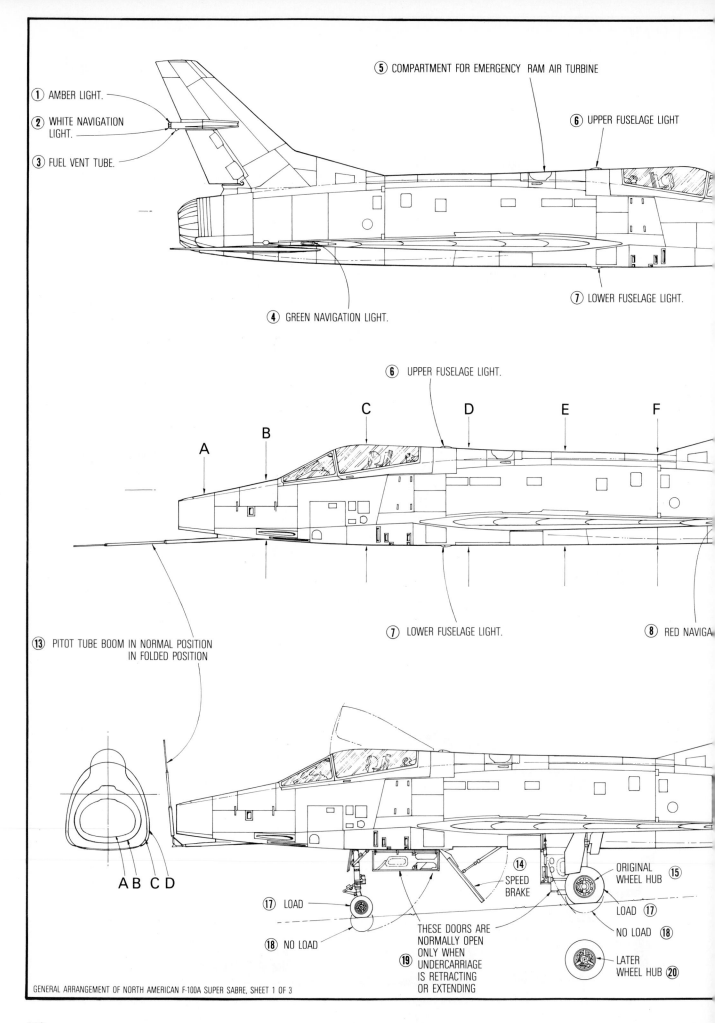

① AMBER LIGHT.

② WHITE NAVIGATION LIGHT.

③ FUEL VENT TUBE.

⑤ COMPARTMENT FOR EMERGENCY RAM AIR TURBINE

⑥ UPPER FUSELAGE LIGHT

⑦ LOWER FUSELAGE LIGHT.

④ GREEN NAVIGATION LIGHT.

⑥ UPPER FUSELAGE LIGHT.

A B C D E F

⑦ LOWER FUSELAGE LIGHT.

⑧ RED NAVIGA

⑬ PITOT TUBE BOOM IN NORMAL POSITION
   IN FOLDED POSITION

A B C D

⑭ SPEED BRAKE

ORIGINAL WHEEL HUB ⑮

⑰ LOAD

LOAD ⑰

NO LOAD ⑱

⑱ NO LOAD

⑲ THESE DOORS ARE NORMALLY OPEN ONLY WHEN UNDERCARRIAGE IS RETRACTING OR EXTENDING

LATER WHEEL HUB ⑳

GENERAL ARRANGEMENT OF NORTH AMERICAN F-100A SUPER SABRE, SHEET 1 OF 3

PLATE 3

NORTH AMERICAN F-100A SUPER SABRE
SIDE AND FRONT ELEVATIONS, AND CROSS SECTIONS

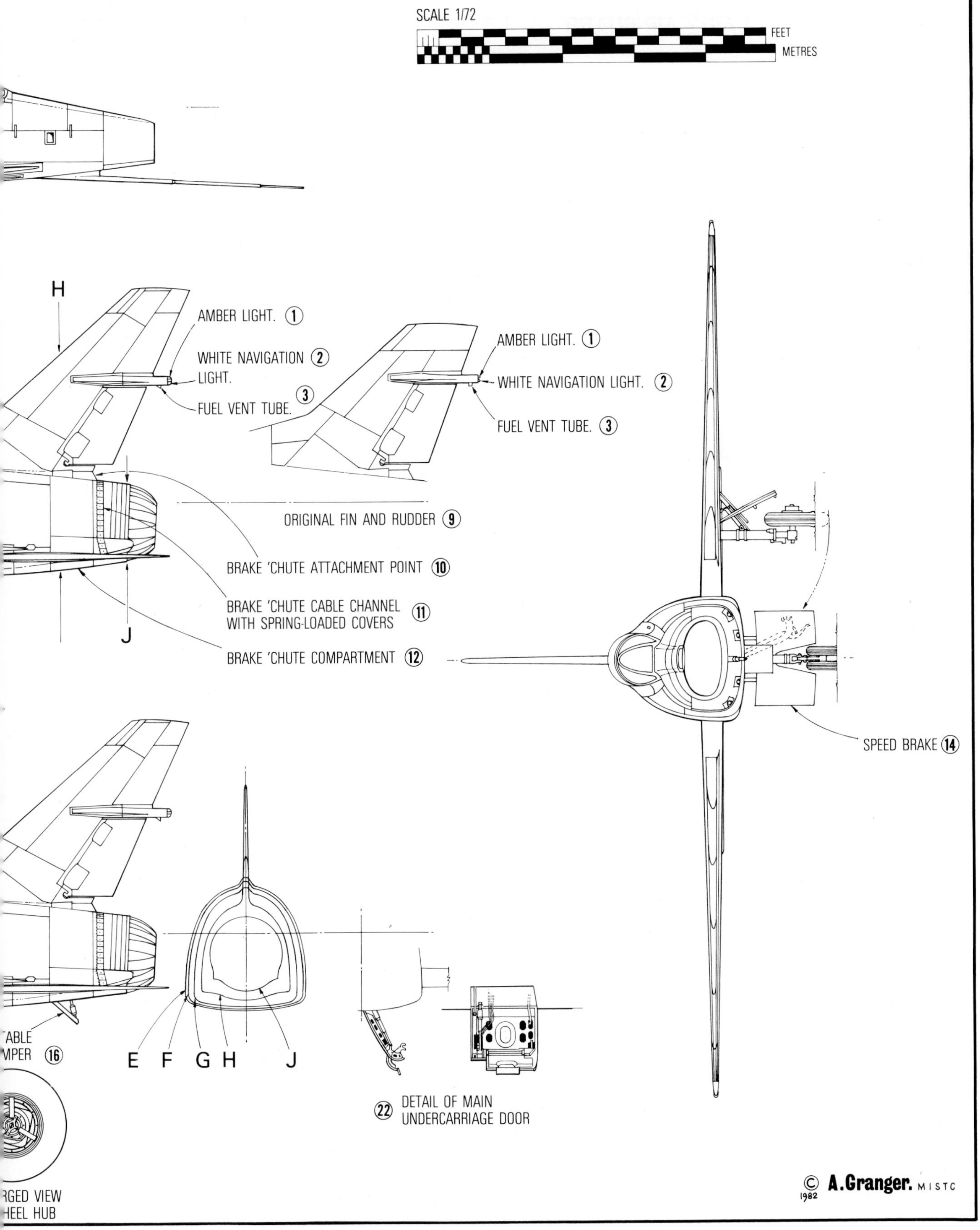

SCALE 1/72
FEET
METRES
H
AMBER LIGHT. ①
WHITE NAVIGATION ② LIGHT.
FUEL VENT TUBE. ③
AMBER LIGHT. ①
WHITE NAVIGATION LIGHT. ②
FUEL VENT TUBE. ③
ORIGINAL FIN AND RUDDER ⑨
BRAKE 'CHUTE ATTACHMENT POINT ⑩
BRAKE 'CHUTE CABLE CHANNEL WITH SPRING-LOADED COVERS ⑪
J
BRAKE 'CHUTE COMPARTMENT ⑫
SPEED BRAKE ⑭
ABLE
MPER ⑯
E F G H J
㉒ DETAIL OF MAIN UNDERCARRIAGE DOOR
RGED VIEW
HEEL HUB
© 1982 A.Granger. MISTC

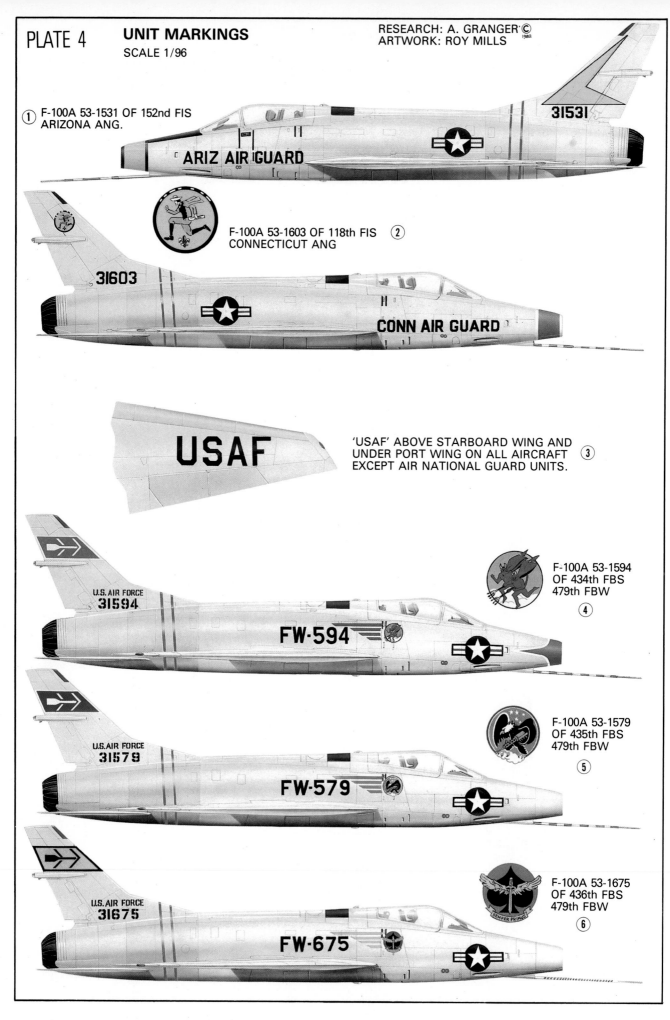

PLATE 4

UNIT MARKINGS
SCALE 1/96

RESEARCH: A. GRANGER©
1982
ARTWORK: ROY MILLS

1. F-100A 53-1531 OF 152nd FIS ARIZONA ANG.

31531

ARIZ AIR GUARD

2. F-100A 53-1603 OF 118th FIS CONNECTICUT ANG

31603

CONN AIR GUARD

USAF

3. 'USAF' ABOVE STARBOARD WING AND UNDER PORT WING ON ALL AIRCRAFT EXCEPT AIR NATIONAL GUARD UNITS.

4. F-100A 53-1594 OF 434th FBS 479th FBW

U.S. AIR FORCE 31594

FW-594

5. F-100A 53-1579 OF 435th FBS 479th FBW

U.S. AIR FORCE 31579

FW-579

6. F-100A 53-1675 OF 436th FBS 479th FBW

U.S. AIR FORCE 31675

FW-675

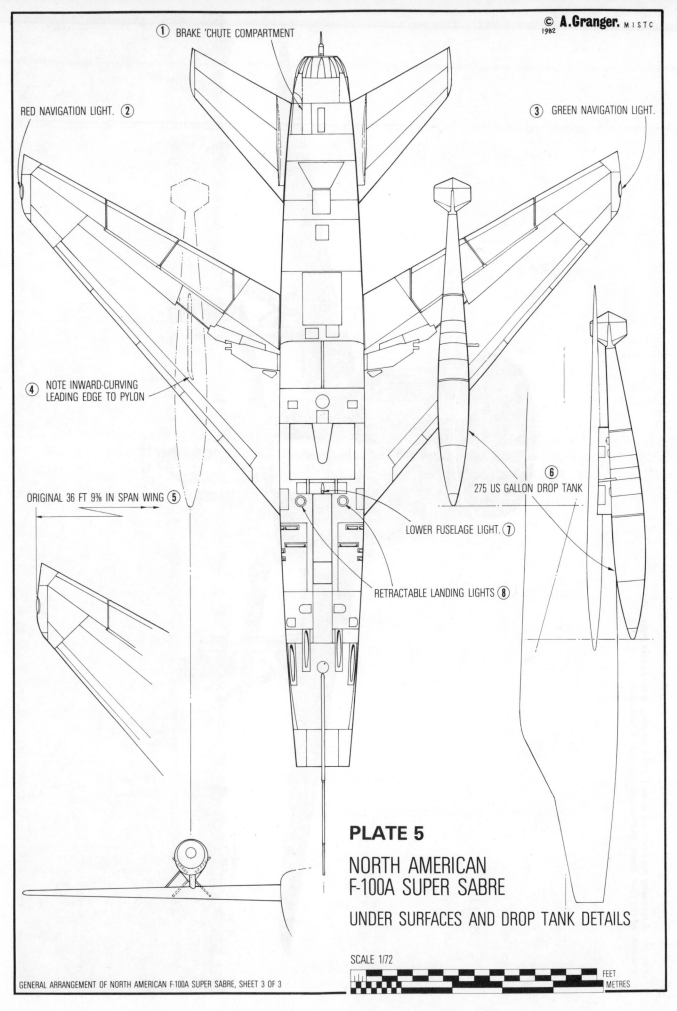

① BRAKE 'CHUTE COMPARTMENT

② RED NAVIGATION LIGHT.

③ GREEN NAVIGATION LIGHT.

④ NOTE INWARD-CURVING LEADING EDGE TO PYLON

⑤ ORIGINAL 36 FT 9⅜ IN SPAN WING

⑥ 275 US GALLON DROP TANK

⑦ LOWER FUSELAGE LIGHT.

⑧ RETRACTABLE LANDING LIGHTS

PLATE 5

NORTH AMERICAN F-100A SUPER SABRE

UNDER SURFACES AND DROP TANK DETAILS

SCALE 1/72

FEET
METRES

GENERAL ARRANGEMENT OF NORTH AMERICAN F-100A SUPER SABRE, SHEET 3 OF 3

Fig. 14 A revealing head-on view of an F-100A showing, among other things, the positions of the four 20mm M-39 canon. (Gordon S Williams)

Fig. 15 *The first production F-100A (52-5756) was the 50,001st aircraft to be delivered by North American. Ninety-eight per cent of the firm's first 50,000 were military aircraft for the US forces and for certain foreign air forces.*

F-100A SPECIFICATION

Powerplant: One Pratt & Whitney J57-P-7 turbojet of 14,500lb (6,576kg) thrust with reheat or, in late production aircraft, one J57-P-39 of 16,000 lb (7,257kg) thrust with reheat.

Dimensions: Span originally 36ft 7in (11,151mm), later 38ft 9⅜in (11,821mm); length with pitot boom folded 47ft 1¼in (14,357mm); height 15ft 6in (4,724.4mm).

Weights: Empty (original A) 19,700lb (8,935.7kg); maximum loaded (original A) 28,935lb (13,120.6kg).

Performance: (with J57-P-7) Maximum speed 852mph (1,371km/h); average cruising speed 589mph (948km/h); service ceiling 44,900ft (13,685m); climb 23,800ft/min (7,254m/min); combat radius 358 miles (576km).

Armament: Four Pontiac-built M-39E 20mm cannon, capable of firing 1,500 rounds per minute, in the lower part of the front fuselage plus under-wing pylons for two 375gal (1,705 litre) fuel tanks and four additional hardpoints for a total of 4,000lb (1,814kg) of ordnance.

equipment from the 104th F-100A onwards, while the final 39 machines had the improved J57-P-39 engine instead of the -7.

A total of 203 F-100As were built before production ceased in favour of the new C model in March 1954. Six were later converted, under the project name *Slick Chick*, into RF-100As carrying reconnaissance cameras in bulging bays on either side of the lower front fuselage.

As improved models of the Super Sabre became available the F-100A was relegated to service with the Air National Guard. Eighty F-100As were upgraded to approximate D model standard and supplied to Nationalist China in 1960 together with a number of F-100F two-seaters.

Fig. 16 *Early production F-100As at North American's Los Angeles, California, plant ready for delivery to the USAF, September 1954.*

Fig. 17 F-100As of the 479th Fighter Day Wing, USAF Tactical Air Command, at George AFB, California. The 479th was the first Air Force Wing to receive Super Sabres, the second being the 450th FDW at Foster AFB, Texas, which received the second version of the Hun — the F-100C.

117

Fig. 18 F-100As of the 479th Fighter Day Wing, George AFB, flash over the Californian Desert at supersonic speeds.

Fig. 19   *Formation flypast by F-100As of the 479th FDW at George AFB.*

119

Fig. 20 *At the end of first-line service many F-100As were relegated to the Air National Guard including the 162nd Fighter Group, Arizona Air Guard, some of whose machines are shown. First two planes are also included in the factory line-up which is the subject of Fig. 16.*

Fig. 21 *One of the six camera-toting RF-100As converted from F-100As under the project name "Slick Chick". Note spurious serial – actually an F-89D serial – and hastily-applied buzz number incorporating an inverted M for a W. (USAF)*

Fig. 22 *Another F-100A flypast scene at George AFB.*